teacher *and* comrade

Richard Dudley, Alan Wieder 2003
(Alan Wieder photographer)

teacher *and* comrade

Richard Dudley and the Fight for Democracy in South Africa

Alan Wieder

State University of New York Press

Published by
STATE UNIVERSITY OF NEW YORK PRESS, ALBANY

Printed in the United States of America

For information, contact State University of New York Press, Albany, NY
www.sunypress.edu

Production and book design, Laurie Searl
Marketing, Michael Campochiaro

Library of Congress Cataloging-in-Publication Data

Wieder, Alan, 1949-
Teacher and comrade : Richard Dudley and the fight for democracy in South Africa / Alan Wieder.
p. cm.
Includes bibliographical references and index.
ISBN 978-0-7914-7429-7 (hardcover : alk. paper)
ISBN 978-0-7914-7430-3 (pbk. : alk. paper)
1. Dudley, R. O. (Richard O.), 1924– 2. Teachers—South Africa—Biography. 3. Human rights workers—South Africa—Biography. 4. Democracy—South Africa. 5. Social movements—South Africa. I. Title.

LA2388.S62D838 2008
371.10092—dc22
[B] 2007034471

10 9 8 7 6 5 4 3 2 1

contents

acknowledgments

First, I would like to thank the South African educators who shared their stories: Richard Dudley's students, colleagues, and comrades; some who adore him, others who are critical, and some who are both. Thank you for inviting me into your homes, schools, and lives. In the United States Craig Kridel, Bob Schwartz, Louise Jennings, Bill Ayers, Wayne Urban, Nadine Dolby, and Roberta Wollons continue to read my work, criticize it, and make it better. Even more critical, but every bit as supportive, are my South African colleagues and comrades. Peter Kallaway and Crain Soudien have mentored me since I first arrived in Cape Town in 1999, and the readings of Aslam Fataar and Azeem Badroodien have been an invaluable part of writing *Teacher and Comrade*.

I am also indebted to the Fulbright Commission, the University of the Western Cape, and my home institution, the University of South Carolina. Fulbright supported me in 1999 and 2005 as I worked on the book. The University of the Western Cape gave me an academic home in South Africa, and the University of South Carolina supported my work in more ways than I can acknowledge. The University provided financial support and a sabbatical, but most important were colleagues and administrators in the College of Education who covered for me during my five extended stays in South Africa since 1999.

Needless to say, I am indebted to Richard Dudley's family: Iris, Gary, and Russell. They have generously shared their lives, and Iris has put up with me being in her home endlessly for many, many years. Thoughts of being in the Dudley home, Tintagel, bring warmth to my heart. Finally, there is no book without Richard Dudley. While I sometimes disagree with him, I admire him, respect him, and adore him. I thank him profusely for allowing me to enter his life.

1

introduction

Before Dudley: Oppression, Racism, and the Roots of Resistance

Much has been written about the fight against apartheid in South Africa, and now, with a continuing flow of publications on the Truth and Reconciliation Commission hearings, we are presented with a unique expanse of stories from the ground. Richard Dudley is one of the fighters. He is an urban educator and political activist who combined foundational ideological politics with great caring, communication, and even compromise as a teacher and nominal principal at Livingstone High School, a highly rated public secondary school that was created for coloured students in 1926. In addition to teaching, Dudley worked endlessly, through various political organizations, against apartheid oppression and for a democratic South Africa. Richard Dudley's life offers us multiple lenses for understanding apartheid South Africa. Dudley is truly a public intellectual, and that in itself is an important story. He is also totally and thoughtfully entwined with the life of Livingstone—first as a student, then as a teacher/principal, and presently as an elder. Finally, Richard Dudley has given his life to teaching and politics and affected and influenced thousands of people who continue to work for democracy in South Africa and abroad.

Dudley's life is totally entwined with education and politics, Livingstone High School, Cape Town, and democracy in South Africa. Dudley's biography gives us the chance to explore the connection of education and politics in Cape Town as he and his comrades challenged first oppression and then apartheid. Dudley was born in 1924 and his story takes us through the many twentieth-century changes in South African oppression and resistance. In addition, we are afforded a picture of both the city, Cape Town, and the country, South Africa, and their resistance education and politics. First and foremost, however, Richard Dudley is a teacher. The thread that runs through his life, chronologically as well as in his many roles, is that he is always teaching. Whether it was at home, at Livingstone High School, in the political organizations where he worked, interacting with political adversaries or government officials, or even when he was detained, Dudley was a teacher.

Teacher with the Fighting Spirit: Noncollaboration and Nonracialism

The pedagogy and politics of Richard Dudley and his comrades have two foundational stands that are written in stone—noncollaboration and nonracialism. Both ideological positions existed before the apartheid regime came to power in 1948, remained during apartheid, and continue in both the beliefs and actions of Dudley and his comrades at the present time. Both stands are important to Dudley's fight for a democratic South Africa and are central to each chapter of his story. Franz Fanon's thesis in *Black Skins White Masks* presents a theoretical perspective for the noncollaboration ideology and action of Dudley and other South Africans. Fanon writes of colonials who take on the white supremacist ideology and actions of the colonialists to oppress other colonials. Isaac Tabata analyzes the theme through South African teachers in *Education for Barbarism*. He also introduces teachers like Dudley who lived and taught noncollaboration and nonracialism.

When I interviewed University of Cape Town history professor William Nasson, who had been a student at Livingstone in the 1960s, he spoke of Dudley with respect and admiration. While Nasson's 1990 article in *Radical History Review*, "The Unity Movement: Its Legacy in Historical Consciousness," is critical of the Unity Movement, it positively provides a context for Dudley and his Teachers' League comrades, "teachers with the fighting spirit." Nasson's recollection is of teachers, whether their subject were language, history, science, or math, providing historical and political analysis with "an influential independent socialist force." He begins his article by quoting one of his teachers.

> This school has a mission to teach you history which will liberate you. We are here to make sure that you aren't contaminated by the Herrenvolk poison contained in your textbook. We as the oppressed cannot afford colonized minds. Our history, our liberation are inseparable. Because it teaches us that we should never salaam before this country's rulers. (Nasson, 1990, p. 189)

Dudley defined his role as a teacher broadly, connecting academic discipline, nonracialism, social class, and world imperialism in his mission. He is quick to argue that the critiques of other left opposition, including Tabata in 1961, and scholars both miss the breadth and depth of Unity Movement teachers. Dudley explains that the population of South Africa was only about 10 million when the apartheid regime came to power, and there was great need to spread liberation ideas—*teacher* did not mean "classroom" but rather corresponded to the "vectors" of ideas.

> All of us involved in the political movement are in fact teachers. Not teachers in the narrow sort of professional sense. We were looking at previous critical changes in human society. The inescapable thing was that there were always people who were thinkers working out, working over, the nature of the events that were occurring and how peoples' actions were influenced by what they heard collectively or what they thought up individually. Particularly we were looking at those things that brought about the transformation from feudal society to bourgeois democracy to the industrialized nations. The separation of the different functions in society—those who are ruling, the separation of powers and so on. We worked over events and abstracted the vital things that people needed to know. (Dudley Interview, 2001)

Noncollaboration was a position that was solidified in the late 1930s and early 1940s before the apartheid government came to power. Noncollaboration was relevant in both education and politics. Nonwhite teachers were somewhat privileged in relationship to other South African people of color, and many failed to question the oppression and racism that existed in society and schools. Fanon analyzes the issue as part of the colonial practice of divide and rule, a tactic that is often critiqued by Dudley and his comrades in regard to both pre-apartheid and apartheid racism and oppression and is currently part of the postcolonial literature on slavery in South Africa. Dennis Ntomela, an African teacher who taught in his rural homeland in the 1980s before moving to Cape Town, experienced black teachers doing colonialist work. He was deeply affected because so many of his fellow teachers honored white people and demeaned black people, including their students. "And we were black and I couldn't understand. Uh, they would say something like, you know, black people are noisy, black people are lazy, black people are careless, and all those negative things would be said at pupil assemblies in the morning as school starts" (Ntombela Interview, 1999). Ntombela spoke about specific instances where the principal and teachers told the students how much better whites were than blacks, how white students were more disciplined, and how they were better behaved in public. Ntombela challenged colleagues with little success and found himself nurturing student self-esteem.

In addition, there were nonwhite South Africans who participated in the political process in cooperation with the oppressive and racist pre-apartheid government. Noncollaboration was a stand that challenged the government, confronted teachers who did not want to compromise their privilege, and also confronted power-seeking politicians who were referred to as "quislings." Some nonwhite teachers and politicians continued as collaborators during apartheid, yet Dudley and his comrades still believe in noncollaboration today, because the end of apartheid did not bring democratic socialism to South Africa. The correspondence of class disparity and racism was addressed by Dudley in his 1992—Jonas Fred Bosch Memorial Lecture.

> The class struggle and the struggle against racism are parts of one struggle. But the very dynamics of struggle, if it is nourished by the growth of class awareness, awareness of the historic duty that the workers and peasants in this country have to carry out, will promote the class struggle to its prime position in the scale of priorities of the liberation movement. (Dudley, 1992, p. 1)

The second foundational rock, nonracialism, is a tenet that Dudley has held since childhood—a belief that you fight racism all the while knowing that there is no such thing as race. Before addressing nonracialism, it might be instructive to briefly discuss the government ethnic and racial distinctions prior to 1994 in South Africa—a country Archbishop Desmond Tutu refers to as a "pigmentocracy." Long before the apartheid regime came to power in 1948, at the turn of the twentieth century, South Africa made racial distinctions between African, coloured, Indian, and white. Racial definitions were legalized by the apartheid regime, but reading those designations makes for further evidence of the social and political construction of race. Consider how the apartheid regime defined coloured:

1. any person who is not a member of the white group or of the native group; and
2. any woman, to whichever race, tribe, or class she may belong, between whom and a person who is, in terms of sub-paragraph 1, a member of the coloured group, there exists a marriage, or who cohabits with such a person;
3. any white man between whom and a woman who in terms of sub-paragraph 1 is a member of the coloured group, there exists a marriage, or who cohabits with such a woman. (Western, 1996, p. 9)

John Western also writes of testing for racial designations using paper grocery store bags and other absurdities. While there will be questions throughout the text and some messiness surrounding nonracial politics and coloured ethnic identity, suffice it to say that Dudley and his comrades, like the antiracist scholars of the present, believe that race is an artificial social and political construction (Gilroy, 2000). Nonracialism was part of the teaching and politics of Dudley and a primary ideological stand in the fight against apartheid. He reflected on hiring teachers at Livingstone.

> I used to be invited by the principal to interview people who made application to the school. We used to point out to people that although the school now fell under the Coloured Affairs Department; the school had a set of aims, objectives and directions which were very explicit. We used to point out to them that we don't have coloured children at this school; we don't have African children at this school; we don't have Indian children at this school; we have boys and girls. And if you can fit in with the program that we have, and if you feel that you have any prejudices and you can leave them outside at the gate of the school and so on, you'd be welcome. (Dudley Interview, 1999)

Like noncollaboration, the thread of nonracialism is evident throughout the story of Dudley and the struggle against apartheid. His colleague and comrade, Helen Kies, provides a nonracialism mantra. "To counter the rulers' main objective, retribalizing to make their divide and rule policy possible and easier. Our main lesson was we are one human Race. There are no superior, no inferior races." (Kies Interview, 1999)

While Richard Dudley spent thirty-nine years on the faculty of Livingstone High School, his civic and political life stretched beyond the school. As a child he began to learn the lessons of nonracialism from his family—parents, siblings, and aunts. As a teen he was taught the lessons of noncollaboration as he joined in the discussions of the various political fellowships that are part of Cape Town, initially in the New Era Fellowship (NEF) where he was schooled in the anticolonialist politics of the day. As a young teacher he became an active member and then leader of the Teachers' League of South Africa (TLSA) and the Non-European Unity Movement (NEUM), two anti-oppression and antiracist political organizations that stressed noncollaboration and nonracialism. In 1984, in the midst of the struggle years, he retired from teaching and became President of the New Unity Movement (NUM), a reincarnation of NEUM. Now in his eighties, although pleased by the collapse of apartheid, Dudley still fights for equality and the democratic world that he believes has yet to come to South Africa.

White Supremacy and Resistance, 1900–1924

Before presenting the outline of the text, it is important to broadly consider the history of oppression and racism that occurred just before Dudley was born that greatly defines twentiety-century South Africa. While Cape Town is unique in reference to the rest of the country, at the time of the South African War at the beginning of the twentieth century it was the most densely populated area of South Africa. Both the government and many white South Africans endorsed class, ethnic, and racial divisions at the time. In 1899, just before the South African War, the British High Commissioner in South Africa, Sir Alfred Milner, exclaimed that "the ultimate end is a self-governing white community, supported by well-treated and justly-governed black labour from Cape Town to Zambesi" (Thompson, 2000, p. 144). As we will see later in the chapter, however, resistance, both black and white, existed throughout the country—including Cape Town.

> The state provided the stepping-stones for whites, both English and especially Afrikaans-speaking, to take power and entrench a system of racially based dominance that was unique in its rigidity. Segregation to 1948, and apartheid afterwards, were policies aimed not simply at separating white from black, but at regulating the way in which the indigenous population was drawn into a new society. Economically, blacks were essential as peasants, workers, and farm tenants; politically the settler state tried to exclude them. The country's relative peace for nearly three-quarters of a century was achieved at the cost of deep divisions of power, race, and wealth. White power in South Africa was more efficient and often more uncompromising than in many other colonial contexts. (Beinart, 1994, p. 3)

The legacy of colonialism and slavery in South Africa led to both class disparity and racial segregation as the country entered the twentieth century. The South African Act of 1905 established equal rights for English and Afrikaners and a lesser place for blacks—both Africans and coloureds. While black labor was needed for the mines and other manual work, the government instituted segregation in housing, although this was initially difficult in Cape Town. Blacks migrated to the mines from rural South Africa as well as Mozambique, but both their occupational roles and their housing accommodations were controlled and segregated. The mine companies instituted compounds for African workers and restrictions on their movement and other freedoms. Some 70,000 whites lived in Johannesburg in 1900, yet 100,000 Africans worked in the city's gold mines, producing over 27 percent of the world's gold.

> Racial segregation and discrimination were nevertheless the hallmarks of the industry. On the Rand, as in Kimberley, African men who had homes in the rural areas left their families for several months at a time to earn money on the mines. As in Kimberley, they lived in all-male compounds owned and controlled by the companies, under severe discipline imposed by African foremen

> responsible to white managers. They were clustered together, as many as fifty to a room, where they slept without beds in double-decker concrete bunks. (Thompson, 2000, p. 121)

In Cape Town, where there were no mines and there had been what might be called a more liberal tradition, there were also attempts to segregate the city's approximately 10,000 African people and 70,000 coloureds. Many Africans came to the city to work on the docks and in various maintenance jobs, but like black miners they were quickly forced to live in the segregated, depressed area of Ndebeni under the rationale that their lifestyles might promote the plague. Ironically, the move to Ndebeni protected them from the disease and death when the plague hit. What did not stop was the oppressive view of white officialdom toward people of color. W. J. Simpson was the plague advisor in the Cape, and his racialism exemplifies the divide. "The Africans living in the town were unfit for urban life; the poorer coloured people were even dirtier in their habits, while the Malays and Indians possessed the habits of the Asiatic, and the poorer-class Portuguese, Italians, Levantines and Jews were almost as filthy as the others" (Bickford-Smith, van Heyningen, Wordon, pp. 18, 19). Segregation was not as easy in Cape Town because Africans began to declare squatter rights at the time, and coloured people were more infused in the city. There was some resistance and poor people, white and black, did live in certain neighborhoods together. However, class disparity also served to segregate coloureds and whites.

In 1910 the country became the Union of South Africa, and the divisions between whites and blacks solidified with laws such as the Native Land Act (1913) that reserved close to 80 percent of the land for whites. Sol Plaatje, one of the founders of the African National Congress (ANC), reacted to the law in his book, *Native Life in South Africa*: "Awaking on Friday morning, June 20, 1913 the South African native found himself, not actually a slave, but a pariah in the land of his birth" (Plaatje, 1916, p. 6). Restrictions were also imposed in the cities, including pass laws for Africans and housing covenants where deeds restricted homes in certain areas to white-only residency. Saul Dubow analyzes early twentieth-century segregation in South Africa and makes connections to industrialization and capitalism. His work is important because he reminds us of the complexities of class and race in the country. While giving credit to other South African historians who connect class and race, such as Shula Marks, William Beinart, and Martin Leggasick, Dubow explains that South African segregation moved from informal and theoretical to political and hegemonic during the formation of the Union. Vivian Bickford-Smith argues that Cape Town was part of the change. He explains that there were Africans living in the city in 1910, that the city was greatly segregated, and that the first example of forced removals preceded the declaration of the Union of South Africa (Bickford-Smith, 2001). The caveat was that there were still areas where whites and blacks lived together. Poor people, both black and white, lived in the neighborhood that became known as District Six, for example, Dudley was born in Newlands, which is presently an elite neighborhood that is sometimes referred to as "millionaires mile," where at that time his neighbors were both white and coloured. These neighborhoods were exceptions, however, and segregation was the South African norm throughout the twentieth century.

The political and legal solidification of segregation had both conservative and liberal rationales. As we review sources, it is difficult to sort class theory from racial hatred and fear. Dubow argues that both conservative and liberal politicians tried to explain the humanity behind the division of the races and talked of laws that simply supported different cultures. Of course, this did not address economic and political ploys of divide and rule. Nor did it address white working-class economic and racist fears or lessen the fact that the government passed legislation that took land from Africans and forced them into becoming cheap wage laborers. Dubow does clearly point out that there were contradictions, and some of them come out in corresponding paragraphs in political speeches and bureaucratic documents, first couched in the liberal racism of "anthropological" differences between black and white and then within the overt conservative portrayal of the depravity of blacks.

Beinart provides examples of racist violence in both the country and the city and also presents government ideological statements that are a foreshadowing of some of the most vicious racist declarations by Hendrik Vervoerd during apartheid.

> The Chamber developed an argument to suggest that if Africans earned more, they would work less. It was based on the assumption that migrant workers with land had only a very limited desire for "luxuries" or consumer items: "the only pressing need of a savage are those of food and sex" so the Labour Commission opined, "and the conditions of Native life in Africa are such that these are as a rule easily supplied." (Beinart, 1994, p. 66)

Segregation meant both exclusion and oppression for African and coloured South Africans. Like the apartheid government that was yet to rise, the Union of South Africa recognized coloureds as above Africans but definitively not equal to whites. Early on the mines reserved certain jobs for whites, and the government and other enterprises had restrictive employment codes just as the apartheid regime would enact when it came to power. For example, many postal and railroad positions were only available to white South Africans. In 1905 Cape Town initiated compulsory primary education for white children, blacks need not apply.

Racial discrimination in jobs, housing, education, and the vote for all people did bring on resistance, and both blacks and whites challenged racism. Shula Marks as well as Beinart and Dubow, however, argue that resistance was not uniform and was actually rather messy. Africans responded to racialism in the mines and other job sites. Although there were strikes and boycotts, African and coloured leadership did not always represent resistance. For example, Tengo Jabavu, an African leader in the Cape, presided over meetings and protests, but he was also worried about alienating powerful whites. He worked with other Africans and formed a team with John Dube, Solomon Plaatje, Pixley kaIsaka Seme, and others to launch the South African Native National Congress (SANNC), the forerunner of today's presiding political party, the African National Congress (Beinart, 1994, pp. 84, 85; Rive & Couzens, 1993). Seme made a powerful speech at the initial conference in 1912.

> Chiefs of royal blood and gentleman of our race, we have gathered here to consider and discuss a theme which my colleagues and I have decided to place before you. We have discussed that in the land of their birth, Africans are treated as hewers of wood and drawers of water. The white people of this country have formed what is known as the Union of South Africa—a union in which we have no voice in the making of laws and no part in their administration. We have called you therefore to this conference so that we can together devise ways and means of forming our national unity and defending our rights and privileges. (Rive & Couzens, 1993, p. 10)

While there were protests and pass burnings and more, the initial resistance is generally considered gradualist in nature, although as Dubow asserts in his recent book on the ANC, the original American and English educated leaders of the organization were committed to "overcoming inter-African ethnic divisions and to extending citizenship and franchise rights to all South Africans on a non-racial basis" (Dubow, 1989. p. 3). As Marks and others have already informed us, however, conservatism and resistance often coexisted. In the initial years through the early 1920s there was geographical diversity in SANNC theory and practice. Leaders in the Transvaal attempted to form alliances with socialist labor and the South African Communist Party. Meanwhile, people such as Solomon Plaatje in the Cape, who on other occasions had written articles and made speeches that were socialist in nature, apologized to Debeers, the diamond company, for the "Johannesburg socialist propaganda" (Meli, 1998, p. 61). Even in the early years, however, the ANC forerunner was the one political organization that preached what today is referred to as multiculturalism.

> They retained a liberal belief in multiracial civilization and citizenship in South Africa. Aside from some white liberals and later socialists, they were the only political grouping at the time to articulate this goal. Their interpretation of non-racialism and their strategies

> for achieving it were often uncertain, as was their view about incorporating the uneducated masses. But they were not offering a black version of exclusive white South Africanism—whites as well as blacks were part of the nation. (Beinart, 1994, p. 89)

The mix of conservatism, liberalism, and socialism that was part of African opposition to Union racism and oppression is evident throughout black resistance, including the coloured political and educational organizations that were founded in Cape Town.

White Supremacy and Coloured Resistance, 1900–1924

The most influential coloured leader at the time the Union of South Africa was formed was Abdullah Abdurahman, who led the African Political Organization (APO) from 1905 until his death in 1940. He was viewed as too outspoken by some other coloured leaders, and their views partially explain the contradictions and the messiness of coloured resistance at the time of Union just before Richard Dudley was born. Abdurahman was a medical doctor, and he was sometimes fiery as he challenged racist policy. As I have noted above, there was a tone of liberalism in the Cape when compared to other parts of South Africa. Cape Town was unique because coloured people who conformed to Cecil Rhodes's slogan of "equal rights for every civilized man south of the Zambesi" were allowed limited franchise. This meant that coloured men who were educated and owned property could vote, but they could not hold office except at the most local levels. Abdurahman, for example, was on the Cape Town city council for four decades. The African Political Organization, with Abdurahman as its leader and spokesman, began in the Cape and grew into a national organization before the Union was formed in 1910. The membership list, however, was primarily from the Cape. Initially in 1902, the APO listed the following mission: (1) To promote unity between the coloured races; (2) To obtain better and higher education for our children; (3) To defend the Coloured People's social, political, and civil rights; (4) To get the names of all coloured men who have voting qualifications; and (5) The general advancement of coloured people in South Africa.

Like Marks, Beinhart, and Dubow; historians of coloured South African history; Gavin Lewis, Ian Goldin, Mohamad Adhikari, and Ciraj Rassool are quick to point out the complexities of coloured politics and resistance. Lewis goes to great length to juxtapose the fight against white supremacy with middle-class white values. In fact, he uses first-person quotes as he continually references coloured leaders who accept Rhodes's edict of "civilized men."

> The APO intended, he declared (Collins), to show the government that there existed "an educated class of Coloured people in Cape

> Town," who could no longer be treated as part of an undifferentiated mass of "uneducated barbarians." The time had come, Collins claimed, for "civilised" Coloureds in all four colonies to receive the rights due to all civilized men. (Lewis, 1987, p. 23)

The APO and specifically Abdurahman also spoke to the rights of all black people. There were statements and protests against the government importing Chinese labor at the expense of black South Africans, and the organization paid persistent attention to uplifting coloured people through education and temperance. But the APO was middle class. The organization was made of coloured men—skilled artisans, small retail traders, clerks, teachers, and a few professionals—and most of the issues they addressed, especially education and limited franchise, were with the hope of the integration of coloured people into white South Africa. Abdurahman pointed out his goals, including the improvement of coloured education and the extension of the nonracial franchise throughout the country, shortly after he became APO president in 1905. He built the APO into an important political organization by 1910 while directly fighting for education and the franchise. There was urgency in the fight for education because the Cape government passed the School Board Act in 1905. Legislators began making noise about compulsory primary education for white children in the final years of the nineteenth century, but action was put on hold because of the South African War. In actuality, de facto school segregation had been the reality in the Cape since the 1860s. White children of means went to nondenominational schools, while black and coloured children attended missionary schools that were underfunded and lacked facilities. In spite of this disparity, the state became concerned because coloured school attendance was growing and white children were not keeping pace. Coloured leaders, on the other hand, believed that compulsory education for white children would infringe upon the educational and therefore occupational possibilities for coloured children.

The APO took up the fight, and Abdurahman was dispatched to argue the case before the Colonial Secretary. He was rebuffed at the meeting and was told that primary compulsory education for white children was essential, because (1) black school enrollment had outpaced whites; (2) whites paid more taxes; and (3) the government could not afford compulsory education for both whites and blacks. After the law passed, there was greater inequality as mission schools closed and the number of white schools doubled. Adhikari provides a class analysis that corresponds to the racism in the act and argues that the government needed to train unskilled, semiliterate workers. "There was thus a clear congruence between the ideals of white supremacy and the educational needs of the rapidly developing capitalist economy. Thus, public education was very deliberately extended to all whites and only very selectively made available to blacks" (Adhikari, 1993, p. 22). Abdurahman, however, was lauded for his work and for standing up to white power. So even though the APO was unsuccessful in the battle for equal education, Abdurahman and the organization were the logical choices to lead the fight for extension of limited franchise as Union day approached.

Abdullah Abdurahman often spoke from a nonracial perspective, but he also was a politician, and the attempt to extend limited franchise outside the Cape became an issue of coloured voting. Although his intentions appear to be realism in politics, stressing the rights of coloureds also endeared him to a segment of the coloured community. He moved the APO toward a loose alliance with the Progressive Party in the hope that Cape progressives would support limited franchise at the national level. At the same time he led APO protests and lobbying against job discrimination and for better wages. The organization also worked hard on temperance and education for coloured people as the means to social and economic advancement. Again he represented Rhodes's "civilized man." The actions of the APO were in contrast to the 1906 street protests by coloured working-class people, socialists such as James La Guma, and coloured gangs like the Hanover Street Burglars Club. As the Union of South Africa was born and white supremacy and the color line became more rather than less cemented, the APO and the extended franchise were quickly forgotten by the Progressives. Laws were passed in the first decade of the Union of South Africa that magnified and solidified white supremacy. Included were protective white labor policies and the solidification of school segregation. The South African Native National Congress grew, and there were protests and demonstrations after the 1913 Land Act. Women publicly destroyed their passes and followed Gandhi's lead of passive resistance. While the government continued strategies to divide and rule black people, the great majority of Africans still lived in rural districts and were somewhat unaffected by the actions of SANNC or APO.

The APO continued to question government actions but appeared to be more and more impotent. Abdurahman and the APO tried to address issues after 1910, but as in the years preceding Union, there were not great successes. The organization again tried to figure out which white party might make the best ally. They fought against the designation of Afrikaans, which they viewed as the voice of the oppressor, as an official language, and they continued to urge coloured South Africans towards becoming Rhodes's "civilized man."

> In his conference addresses, Abdurahman advised APO members to show themselves by their conduct and actions, "the equals, physically, morally and intellectually, of whites." Furthermore, he reminded APO members, as the "intelligent section of the Coloured people," of their duty to uplift other Coloureds, whether the "common farm labourer" or the "worst hooligan of the city slums," and make them "become as self-respecting and respectable citizens as we think we are." (Lewis, 1987, p. 73)

Abdurahman also attempted to forge an alliance with SANNC in the early years of the Union. At the 1912 APO conference he argued against coloured racism, but he had to repeat the message at the 1913 conference as he also spoke with great anger and almost a threatening tone about the victory of white supremacy in the country. Union white supremacy had a great effect on the lives of coloured people in Cape Town, and the impotency of the APO spurred dissenters who if anything were even less effective at challenging government racism. Lewis presents data on the changes in Cape Town that include huge drops in the number of coloured professionals during the first years of Union. The exception, however, was teachers. So while the APO became quiet, stopped publishing its newspaper, and curtailed meetings until 1919, a new organization was introduced that would become one of the most important institutions in Richard Dudley's life—the Teachers' League of South Africa (TLSA).

The TLSA was founded June 1913 in Cape Town as an organization for coloured teachers. While the APO appeared to struggle at least minimally with being a coloured or nonracial organization, Mohamed Adhikari argues that the organization "perceived itself as representing the coloured people as a whole and as an institution that had an instrumental role to play in the destiny of this community" (Adhikari, 1993, p. 5). In telling the history of the TLSA between 1913 and 1940, Adhikari analyzes both the colonial oppression that constructed coloured and the identity that was embraced by coloured leaders who reached for assimilation into white South Africa but then settled for coloured rather than African, as the Union of South Africa upped the ante as a white supremacist government. My portrayal of the analysis might be a bit harsh, but what appears very clear is that the TLSA was originally founded as an organization for coloured teachers. The first president of the organization was Harold Cressy, a well-known Cape Town teacher who was among the small number of nonwhites who was able to attend South African College, the school that became the University of Cape Town in 1918. According to Lewis, Abdullah Abdurahman used his position on the Cape Town City Council to gain admittance for Cressy at the white-only institution. In 1911 Harold Cressy became principal of Trafalgar High School, the first colored secondary school in Cape Town. Livingstone High School, Dudley's school, was not founded until 1926. Although Abdurahman remained quiet at the time of the founding of the TLSA, he actually initiated the formation of the League. In fact, in 1934 he publicly stated that the Teachers' League of South Africa was born at a meeting in his home. (Lewis, 1987, p. 35)

The TLSA began as an organization that combined a mission to improve coloured education with a call for pride and responsibility for coloured South Africans. After all, 88 percent of funding went to white education (Lewis, 1987, p. 68). Teachers had a clear understanding of problems in their working conditions that affected the education of the children. Included were (1) low salaries and no pensions, (2) abuse by school managers, and (3) inferior teacher training facilities. While these issues were addressed at conferences and meetings throughout the life of the organization, there was also an immediacy in the fact that the TLSA served as a community and cultural model. Harold Cressy cited both Booker T. Washington and W.E.B. Dubois in the United States as examples of blacks not relying on whites for education and success. The organization represented the solidification of coloured identity and solidarity. There was a distinction made between coloureds and Africans.

> The League also made it clear at the inaugural conference that it regarded Africans to be a group distinct from coloureds and that they needed to minister to their own sectional interests. That the constitution adopted at that gathering gave the main object of the League as the improvement of the education of the "Cape Coloured population" is a clear indication of this. Also, the unanimous acceptance of Cressy's motion calling for the separation of coloured and African educational statistics confirmed the racial exclusivism of the League. (Adhikari, 1993, p. 33)

This is how the Teachers' League of South Africa began a decade before the birth of Richard Dudley. The *Educational Journal*, the voice of the League, was first published in 1915 and provided educational and cultural news, issues and opinions. Included were philosophical discussions, debates, conference proceedings, grievances, curriculum, and model lessons. Shortly after the birth of the TLSA, teachers and other coloured South Africans joined the United Kingdom in the war effort, but from the perspective of coloured leaders, patriotism did not help the fortunes of the group. In 1919 the APO met for the first time in six years. At both that meeting and the 1923 conference, Abdurahman had to repeat his admissions of impotence from 1913. In fact, after World War I coloured South Africans were more deprived economically than earlier in the century, and the government began to pass laws that promoted white employment. The 1921 Juveniles Act legislated helping white youth find work, and the 1922 Apprenticeship Act initiated apprenticeships for young people who completed a Standard Six education. The latter law was a very clear statement because most black schools only went to Standard Five. Abdurahman was blunt when he addressed the 1923 conference. He explained that the actions of white supremacy would eventually lead to "black unity and the expulsion of all whites from Africa." However, in spite of the rhetoric, the APO was in a difficult position because there were few successes. The organization changed its name to the African Peoples Organization as a symbol of less politics and more self-help and communal activities. In 1920 the Cape government passed an Education Ordinance that opened up free primary education for all, although there was a caveat that white children come first. The ordinance was coupled with differentiated curriculums—one for white schools and another for coloured schools. The year before Dudley was born saw the APO stumbling for relevance in white supremacist South Africa. There is some irony because in 1924, the year he was born, there was a push to the left in the African Peoples Organization and coloured politics.

Richard Dudley and the Fight for Democracy

We begin our journey in the fight for democracy in South Africa in the 1920s and 1930s when Dudley was a child and teen. Chapter Two is titled Childhood and Youth: Learning Books, Learning Non-racialism. While the government was extending racist legislation, black South Africans were losing both rights and income. There was continuing resistance with some successes, a lot of failures, and many schisms among organizations and individual resisters. As 1940 approached, a more radical voice of black resistance began to grow in Cape Town. That was the movement that eventually attracted Richard Dudley, at least partially because childhood and youth was a time that his parents and teachers stressed learning. But it was also the beginning of his education in nonracialism through the mentorship of family, neighbors, and Livingstone High School teachers. The 1920s and 1930s was a time in South African history when many other black South Africans, some of whom would become Dudley's colleagues and comrades, began their educations on resisting racism and oppression.

Education and Politics: Lessons for Teaching and Struggle is the third chapter of the book. Although political education began at Livingstone, more sophisticated tutoring occurred at the University of Cape Town and through the New Era Fellowship and other political organizations. Chapter Three examines Dudley's coming of age politically as he studied and connected imperialism and colonialism to South Africa and as he became a student member of the Teachers' League of South Africa, just at the time that The League was radicalizing its politics.

Chapter Four is titled Becoming a Teacher, Becoming a Comrade: Pre-Apartheid Years. As a young teacher at Livingstone High School, the job was to combine academic excellence and politics in order to nurture both student achievement and an understanding of the connections of class and race in South Africa and throughout the world. Dudley, of course, had to adjust to being a new teacher, and he was fortunate to continue to have his own teachers—both older colleagues at the school and comrades in the New Era Fellowship and Teachers' League. As he began his life as a teacher, he also became a full member of both of the above organizations as well as the Non-European Unity Movement. He was bestowed with many responsibilities in each group, including writing, speaking, and various other activities.

Teaching and the struggle for democracy, of course, became the work of Richard Dudley's life. His journey continues into the early years of apartheid up until the time of his banning, portrayed in Chapter Five, Education for Democracy I: The Early Years of Apartheid through Sharpeville, 1948–1960. In the chapter Dudley's work at Livingstone and the TLSA are viewed in correspondence with apartheid legislation and action that solidify and magnify racist oppression. The same issues, although sometimes more covert on the political side, are the subject of Chapter Six, Education for Democracy II: From Bannings to the Soweto. While Dudley's teaching and political work continued, he was affected both publicly and personally by the acceleration and escalation of racism during this time period. Education for (Liberation) Before Education is the title of Chapter Seven. The chapter addresses some of the most difficult times for both Dudley and Livingstone High School. In the late 1970s through the struggle years, Dudley and his comrades continually battled what they viewed as "action for the sake of action." Black consciousness, student activism, and the intensification of apartheid oppression are all part of the struggle years. Chapter Seven describes and analyzes Dudley's place at the time, including his leadership role in the relaunching of the Unity Movement, his retirement from teaching, and his transition to the end of the apartheid era.

The conclusion of the book is called Reflecting on Reflections: Conclusions and Considerations of the Present. Not just a conclusion, it is also a portrait of how, even after the fall of apartheid, Dudley remains critical of the capitalist-imperialist world ethos that South Africa has joined through the World Bank and International Monetary Fund, as well as the continuing class disparity in South Africa. Thus, as Richard Dudley lives in his ninth decade, he continues his foundational belief in nonracialism and finds it necessary to further live a noncollaborationist life. Most importantly, he continues to teach—politically, academically, and in all aspects of life, including telling us his story.

Finally, it is important to ask the so-what question. Why write a book on South Africa through the life of Richard Dudley? As I was working on my oral history project with South African teachers who had fought apartheid, I was scheduled to meet Dudley for the first time in early April 1999. A number of the people I had interviewed, as well as colleagues at both the University of the Western Cape and the University of Cape Town, had emphasized how important Dudley was to education and politics in Cape Town. The night before our first interview, I met with four teachers who had all taught at various black schools in Cape Town. In addition, they had worked together under Dudley at Livingstone High School. As they told me their stories, it was almost as if they were more enthused about my meeting Dudley the following day than actually talking about their lives as teachers. Dudley, however, was part of their stories, just as he has been part of the lives of hundreds of other teachers and thousands of students during his lifetime. Besides their joy as they thought of him, each of the women had something to say about Richard Dudley. Rose Jackson referred to the school as having the "benign Dudley spirit," and Beth Mclagan expanded on the tone Dudley brought to Livingstone.

> You felt that Mr. Dudley valued you as a teacher. You had a strong sense that he wanted you to succeed. That he wanted you to be able to give your best in a relaxed kind of atmosphere. You always thought that he was very much on your side but not anti the kids. But interested in how you're doing, how are things going. I come from a very small school environment, so I was a bit overwhelmed by the sheer number of people at Livingstone. And I didn't feel at all anonymous, I felt very supported. (Mclagan Interview, 1999)

The next day, when I met Richard Dudley, as well as nine years and over 200 hours of interviewing him later, I have never once questioned the assessment I was presented by Pam Dewes, Pam Hicks, Beth Mclagan, and Rose Jackson that Tuesday evening in 1999. After I had completed interviewing more than 50 teachers in 1999, I had about a month left before I was to leave the country to return to the United States. At that point I did not have more interviews in me. I had completed so many and there was work to be done with the transcripts of the teachers who told me their stories. At the same time I was already regretting that I had not sat and listened to Richard Dudley again and again and again. We visited a number of times in October 1999 before I departed Cape Town, and in those conversations there were insights and further understanding of his life as a teacher and his fight for democracy in South Africa. But I did not record; it was not the time. I did leave the country with a promise that I would return and that he would be willing to continue the conversation. So we sat together for many hours in December 2001 and January 2002, and again from December 2002 until May 2003, and finally in May and June 2005. During those times I also completed over a hundred additional hours interviewing Dudley's family, students, colleagues, and comrades. Those meetings convinced me even more that his story as a teacher and political activist adds important understanding of oppression, resistance, politics, education, and most of all the connection between human relationships and the struggle for democracy in South Africa throughout the twentieth century. Richard Dudley's story is unique and significant as part of the literature on apartheid resistance. Hopefully, it will encourage additional portraits of teacher resistance in South Africa and throughout the world.

2

childhood and youth

Learning Books, Learning Nonracialism

In the 1960s, after the apartheid government began to enforce the "group areas act" in Cape Town, Richard Dudley's parents, Samuel and Alleta Dudley, were forcibly removed from their home in Newlands, the home where Richard Dudley was born. Today that house stands at the corner of Palmboom Road and Dudley Lane in the plush suburb of Newlands. Yes, Dudley Lane. While the story is not clear, the ironies and contradictions of life are unquestionable, especially in South Africa before the first democratic election in 1994. When Richard Dudley was born in 1924, it was also a time of massive contradictions. That year saw the election of the PACT government, an alliance of the National and Labour parties that defeated the South African Party, the political party that Abdullah Abdurahman supported in spite of continual disappointments. So while Dudley's parents, aunts, older siblings, and teachers were stressing the importance of books and learning, the South African government was promoting differential curriculums with academics for whites, technical education for coloureds, and almost no education for Africans. While Dudley was learning the lessons of nonracialism, the PACT government was passing legislation to divide the races and oppress black South Africans. This is the world that welcomed Richard Dudley in 1924.

The Pact government came into power at least partially because of the downward turn in the South African economy after the war. The Smuts government had violently crushed the Rand Revolt, a strike by white miners, and Hertzog became Prime Minister on the promise to support and protect white workers. Although he espoused coloured job preference over Africans, much of the promise was a con with only some protection in the Cape. In the first ten years of Dudley's life, Hertzog came through on his promise to white South Africans, promoting white privilege in jobs and education. The railroad became the largest employer of white Afrikaners at the expense of black workers, and the franchise was given to white women, emasculating the coloured vote in the Cape. Between 1924 and 1933 the coloured voter rolls in the Cape Province dropped from 20 percent to 10 percent. Hertzog was able to make Afrikaans an official language, opening up civil service jobs to the Afrikaner population. World War I had a detrimental effect on coloured male employment in Cape Town, while there was a short period in the 1920s when coloured women were employed for low wages in the quickly expanding garment industry. But Hertzog and the Nationalist Party changed policies to favor white women by 1930, and some in the industry, such as A. Fraser and Company in Cape Town, had a whites-only employment policy. During the 1920s Cape Town changed dramatically for its white citizens, but much of the growth was on the back of blacks because of the racist legislation Hertzog initiated. The garment and shipping industries grew, and the economy helped bring electricity, cars, and movies to South Africa.

The year Dudley was born, radio came to South Africa and you could listen to BBC news every evening. The Dudleys did not own a radio until 1939. Cape Town established itself as the cultural capital of the country with the building of the National Gallery. There was certainly progress, but modernity only magnified the country's class and race disparity. Of course there was also inequality in education. While the Education Ordinance of 1920 in the Cape Province provided for primary education for all children, it emphasized different teacher training for white and black teachers and separate curriculums for black and white students.

Dudley's childhood memories are at least partially a Huckleberry Finn or Tom Sawyer existence along the creeks and in the foothills of Cape Town's famous Table Mountain. Dudley's boyhood was spent on the south side of the mountain, and he is quick to assert that as a child the extended neighborhood was what he knew. Interestingly, the well-known local history *Cape Town in the Twentieth Century* describes the Dudley home as having a "garden big enough for a sort of market gardening operation" (Bickford-Smith, van Heyningen, and Worden, 1996, p. 131). Vendors came to the house to sell their wares, and nearby shops provided necessary goods. In addition, the family bartered with neighbors, trading goat's milk for orange juice and mealie stalks for cow manure. The family also gave away fruits and vegetables, although Dudley and his siblings were not ashamed when "on the QT if children offered us a penny for loquats we would accept that penny without telling our parents." But for every capitalist act there was socialist training.

> We used to roam around in Newlands. We used to prance up the rivers and where there were properties abutting on the river with fruit we used to restore our tissues with stolen fruit without much

> consequence because we became quite adept at helping ourselves. That was the first stage I should say of redistributing some of the economic resources in the country. (Dudley Interview, 1999)

Cape Town appeared as a distant urban place only accessible by tram or train. Of course, when he speaks of his teenage years the train ride is anything but problematic. In spite of the many contradictions and the great racial and class disparity in the city, Cape Town was and is an enchanting place, both visually and in the rich diversity of Capetonians. Before I arrived in the city for the first time, I came upon this passage on Table Mountain, a sight that Dudley viewed as a child.

> High above Cape Town, on any otherwise clear day, a snow-white cloud will form, a thin level stripe drawn across the top of the already improbable Table Mountain. Soon the cloud will begin to spill, first in modest cottony puffs, trickling gently over the edge, later in huge silent cataracts, pouring a thousand feet, two thousand feet down the cliffs, as if to inundate the city below. The downward-rushing clouds never reach the city; they burn up as they hit warmer air. But the wave keeps coming, charging off the top of the mountain, out of the strange level cloud, swirling down the great rock face. (Finnegan, 1994, p. 3)

So Richard Dudley grew up on the south side of the mountain, and his memories are of family, neighborhood, and school. He recalls chores around the house such as feeding the chickens, digging and planting and collecting dung from a neighbor's cows for the garden. He remembers a childhood that was both self-contained and expansive, with home as a sanctuary while the street was active, and visitors—friends and family—were in the house quite often. Much of this experience includes an emphasis on education and nonracialism in the shadow of South African pigmentocracy. Dudley provides his own caveat as he speaks about his childhood at the end of his eighth decade: "So what I am going to say is going to be looking back and just hope that in the process I am not romanticizing things and getting too far away from the truth." Yes, one of the never-ending dilemmas of oral history and memory.

The Value of Education

Samuel Dudley, Richard Dudley's father, was the principal of a school in the neighborhood, St. Andrews Mission School, the primary school that Richard Dudley and his siblings attended. There were seven children in the family but the youngest son died in childhood. Eileen, Doris, and Samuel, Jr., were older, and they all trained as teachers. Leonora and Ruth were younger and worked commercially. Dudley explained that because his younger sisters "were not so deeply tanned as their brother, they were able to get relatively well-paid jobs." All of his sisters and his brother eventually left South Africa during apartheid. But they were ever present as children. Dudley's childhood home was a place of education in both music and books. The house sat on a rather large corner lot and was a two-family dwelling. The house was originally purchased in 1852 by his paternal great grandfather and went through his grandfather to his father. Samuel Dudley's sister and her family lived on the other side of the house, and two other aunts often stayed with the family, a condition of inheriting the property. One of those aunts, Maude, figures in both Dudley's book education and lessons of nonracialism. His aunt, uncle, and cousin who lived next door will be introduced as we speak of nonracialism.

While Samuel Dudley was a member of both the African Peoples' Organization and the Teachers' League of South Africa, he was not an active participant. Between teaching and administrating St. Andrews Mission School, working a second job, and seeing to his family, he chose not to spend his time politically. For recreation he met with other men at the neighborhood pub, and their game was darts. But much of his time was spent at home, where Richard Dudley remembers him as strict yet tolerant in a home that was alive and joyful. A large part of family time was spent around the piano singing and visiting with family and the many visitors that came to see both the children and their parents. The piano was a gift from Alleta Dudley's father, and the girls in the family were expected to play. "And we used to listen in when my sisters took their music lessons. In a certain sense that was Victorian, because you remember that in Victorian times it was regarded as an obligation to get the girls to play some musical instrument. In the case of the boys, they could grow up as barbarians and so on because society did not matter."

Actually education mattered a great deal to Richard Dudley's parents. He began reading before entering primary school, and books were part of his childhood just as they are in his ninth decade. His mother watched over his schoolwork after he entered St. Andrews, and his father was strict about his studies. Dudley speaks about books as he recalls his Aunt Maude, the teacher.

> I think that she also brought into the house the books. In addition to that a number of people who my father associated with and who lived in Newlands also gave him books because of the fact that he was a schoolmaster. They gave books for us children. We had a library of books that we could read. I started reading Dickens, for example, and Sir Walter Scott at a fairly early age without really understanding of course, but the books were there. (Dudley Interview, 2001)

Richard Dudley was prepared when he followed his brother Samuel, Jr., to St. Andrews Mission School. The school that his father led was a community school where Samuel Dudley selected teachers because they were strict and knowledgeable. Students attended St. Andrews for the first five years of their schooling. Dudley's recollections are of the classroom, sports, and a huge hall that hosted school and community performances. Samuel Dudley nurtured church and community participation in the school.

> The other thing that I think was very noteworthy was the school was supported by the generosity of people who assisted in one way or another with material, even education material. Members of the congregation formed a kind of backup for the school. Things like, for example, the maintenance of the school, the cleaning up of the school that could not be done by the staff were done largely on a volunteer basis or at minimum cost. (Dudley Interview, 2001)

Dudley did not enter St. Andrews at the traditional age, and of course there is a story. He spent his primary years at the school and then enrolled in Livingstone after completing Standard 4, or Grade 6. He began St. Andrews at the same time as Samuel, Jr., who was almost two years his senior.

> When he was sent to school I insisted on going with him. My mother and my father told me exactly what happened. Apparently when I noticed that he was going to school I said that I wanted to go to school. And when they told me that I could not go to school I created one hell of a scene and they reckoned that the only way they could shut me up was to allow me to go, and that is how I landed in school. And although I was not supposed to be there the teacher allowed me to sit in the class, and they found out that I could manage what the other pupils were doing. I was four when I went to Sub A as it was called, or Grade 1. I just continued in that way, and at the end of the year they thought that I was sufficiently capable of handling the numbers and words and reading, and so I went on to Sub B. (Dudley Interview, 2001)

The importance of education is reflected in Dudley's memories of his teachers, subjects, and the books he read in the primary grades. Prayers and hymns were sung in the morning and subjects included math, language, geography, history, and hygiene. There was also memorization, and Dudley rather humorously argues the necessity of the need for routine, using memorizing telephone numbers as an example and explaining that there are not too many people called Newton or Einstein. Besides basics in numbers and language, schooling included learning through books like *Britain and Her Empire.*

Dudley reports reading *Robinson Crusoe*, *The Last of the Mohicans*, and *Peter Pan*, but he explains that choice of books depended on what happened to be available in the numbers needed. Upon reflection he remembers committed and caring teachers and being prepared to enter Livingstone.

Livingstone High School is foundational in telling the story of Richard Dudley. Imagine attending a school for six years, student teaching at the school for a year, and then spending thirty-nine years teaching at the same school—forty-six years in one institution. Livingstone High School was founded in 1926, two years after Dudley was born. Although there were public high schools for white students at the time, there was only one high school, Trafalgar, serving coloured students. There were at least thirteen mission schools in the Claremont, Lansdowne, and Newlands area but no high school. Livingstone was started by coloured leaders, including Abdullah Abdurahman, to provide a high school education for coloured students who lived on the south side of Table Mountain. The school sits on Lansdowne Road on a site that was originally a dairy farm. In fact, the original school was in the farm stables and is still referred to as "The Stables." In the early years the school often rented space in nearby buildings and at one point held classes for senior students in tents. The curriculum when Dudley entered Livingstone included language, science, math, history, art, music, drama, physical education, and for a short time agricultural science. Dudley's years as a student at the school were essential to his academic learning as well as his learning nonracialism. We will conclude the section with a discussion of Dudley's academic experiences at the school.

When Dudley entered Livingstone he was only nine years old, and most of his classmates were two years older. The age difference had also been the case at St. Andrews, but in primary school the children were all from his community so there was warmth and comfort. Livingstone attracted students from a larger area, and age and size made him somewhat apprehensive when he started his classes. The school was definitely tracked before the word became an educational term, and Dudley began with his brother in a midlevel section of Standard Five. Dudley was with students from other sections of town, and he was not with the best and the brightest. Both of these conditions might have raised his anxiety. However, after his first exams he was promoted to the highest academic class, and that continued to be his experience throughout his years at the school. Livingstone High School went through a number of transformations during Dudley's student years. Additions were added to the building as the student population grew. The growth began in earnest in 1936, as jobs became scarcer for blacks and parents saw a greater need for a high school education for their children—especially girls. There was also a change over this short time in the faculty at the school. Three coloured women, Milly Kay, Ray Carlier, and Naomi Solomon, all with university degrees, joined the staff as did others who were left wing; thus in at least a small way began Dudley's political education.

Richard Dudley speaks with great respect for his teachers at Livingstone. He remembers lessons, classes, readings and a tone of the importance of education as teachers pushed students towards higher education. As already noted, there was tracking at the school, and there are critiques of Livingstone in later years as only serving the needs of the academically talented. Dudley, however, remembers teachers preparing students for the apprenticeship exams they would take after leaving school upon completing Standard 6.

> What I am trying to convey is that there was a spirit of dedication amongst the teachers that I think meant a hell of a lot in maintaining the interest of the school and actually also providing some kind of way forward. The lads who might have had difficulty, if they did well in mathematics, in science, they could in fact compete for apprenticeships in the Simonstown dockyard, because the British at that time opened up their entrance examinations to all persons. We were all British subjects although some of us by South African standards were British objects. (Dudley Interview, 2003)

But again, Dudley's experience was of a highly academic setting with a political edge during his senior years. He speaks of teachers exciting students about literature and history and numbers and science. However, as he began the senior level of the school with a bursary from the Cape Town city council, his curriculum stressed language, science, and math. "I did not take history. They used to give history to the pupils who were less academic. And then they used to give physiology and hygiene to the pupils who took history. And for us who were supposed to have a little more brain matter they gave us Latin, physical science, biology, and geography" (Dudley Interview, 2002). He reread *Robinson Crusoe* with Christine Brear in Standard 5, and the class "lit a flame in reading." Egypt came alive through the teaching and readings of Milly Kay as did the battles between Elizabeth and Mary in England. In Standard 7 the book, *The Path of the King*, by John Buchan, stands out because it explores the British royalty and genes and heredity.

In Standard 8 he took both English and Latin with Muriel Ward, and his class read a good amount of Charles Dickens. He also recalls rigor in Afrikaans with Jooste. During his Standard 9 year leftist teachers joined the staff; Arthur Davids was a member of the socialist Fourth International, and Allie Fataar and Frank Grammer were part of the new wave in the Teachers' League of South Africa. In addition, two women, Dora Douglas and Joyce Ruskin, were Jewish and also had left leanings. Dudley had classes with Davids, Douglas, and Ruskin. He refers to Ruskin, with whom he took math, as a "Trojan woman" who pushed him in math and science, but his memories of Douglas and Davids are more descriptive—both pedagogically and politically. Douglas taught Sophocles and Euripides, poetry, Shakespeare, and introduced a special course on the history of language for university-bound students; she knew that it was part of the first-year curriculum at the University and she wanted her students to be prepared. But Dudley's reflections of English class with Dora Douglas focus on the teacher: "And there was a woman who drove us really hard. Now you can read that, you know, as a sort of mythological type of thing, or you could read it with the kind of insights that a good English teacher can give you. I think that was the big difference that we felt." Dudley and his fellow students also learned a great deal about European and world politics from both Ruskin and Douglas, because each woman had relatives who were being threatened by the Nazis at the time. From Ruskin it was personal.

> I can remember Miss Ruskin going to listen to a radio that they had in the staff room. The Germans had bombed Warsaw, and she came running into our math class. She was as red as a turkey, and she just burst out that they were bombing Warsaw. Now that was an explosion in our sort of understanding of what was happening. We might have been talking about it, Mussolini and so on, but we were not in the history section. And this was just the sort of thing that we learned. Talking from a personal point of view, I think I sat up because we were very fond of Miss Ruskin, and to see her in this state of distress made us almost weep. (Dudley Interview, 2002)

Douglas used a book called *Address Unknown* by Katherine Kressmann Taylor that had a great effect on Dudley and his classmates because it recorded correspondence of people in Europe with friends in the United States as Nazi genocide began. The title is a metaphor for a letter that is returned to someone in the United States marked "address unknown," meaning, of course, that the person in Europe has been taken to a concentration camp. Dudley remembers Douglas teaching them of Jews who came to Cape Town from Germany, Poland, and Lithuania. "What I can remember was a development of a picture that was becoming more and more severe for people overseas. She got that from her books, and we got that from her." (Dudley Interview, 2002)

Tippy Davids, as his political comrades called him, provided breadth to the Livingstone curriculum. In Latin class, students studied Roman institutions as well as culture, and they made oral presentations—short lectures to the class—an innovation at the time. Davids introduced students to education outside of the school. He took his students to the University of Cape Town to meet the botanist Eddie Roux who was doing groundbreaking research on rehabilitating farmlands that had been destroyed through native land policy towards Africans. Roux was a political activist and later wrote *Time Longer than Rope*, a history of the struggles against racism in South Africa. On a different occasion Davids accompanied students to a talk by Ramakrishna at the University. There were other outside activities supported by the school. Teachers sometimes went with students to plays, and the school sponsored debates with other institutions. Dudley recalls a thrashing by students from Zonnebloem, an Anglican school in Cape Town. Ray Carlier organized visits and mutual programs with other schools, including some in rural areas, and of course there were school sports.

Dudley and some of the other students at the top of their class also participated in student council and the prefect system. Student council members organized events and acted as guides for students in the younger grades. In fact, when he was in Grade 11, Richard Dudley was assigned to a ninth-grade class where he met Iris Atkins, his future wife. Prefects also had a disciplinary role helping to keep order at the school. In his final year at Livingstone, Dudley was the head boy prefect, a position where he worked with teachers and also served to monitor fellow students.

Throughout Dudley's student years at Livingstone and up until 1952, the principal was Edward Roberts, and he clearly put his stamp on the school. He monitored both teachers and students and set a tone that was both educational and political. One thing that is very clear is that students like Dudley were supposed to excel and make the school and community proud. This is an intriguing concept because analysis of the school in later years by both historians and some Livingstone students is critical of the school for catering to the academically talented at the expense of other students. A corresponding issue that has also been critiqued is that high schools like Livingstone, Harold Cressy, Trafalgar, and South Peninsula cared more about nurturing professionals than fighting apartheid. The leaders of Livingstone High School believed that they should have a large say in what Dudley and other top students did with their lives. In 1938 the school committee still included most of the same people who helped found Livingstone in 1926. The school had already been successful in bringing graduates like Allie Fataar back as teachers, and they were determined to continue the practice. Dudley had decided to study English and history at the University of Cape Town, but he was not clear on how his education would be funded. His father had sought advice from one of his billiard mates who taught at the University, J. G. Taylor, who later became a political comrade of Richard Dudley's. Taylor opined that Dudley should spend some time selling newspapers or the like to gain the experiences of the streets. Of course this was not really a possibility, nor was studying English and history. Dudley and other students who excelled in their coursework were called to meet with the school committee. They were informed that they would receive bursaries to study at the University, but they were also informed of what they would study: " 'We are telling you that you are going to do science. We have noticed that you have done very well in all our subjects, but we would like you to do science so that you could come back to Livingstone and teach science and mathematics.' So that was not just a suggestion. It was final." (Dudley Interview, 2002)

Learning was ever-present for Richard Dudley in his home, at St. Andrews Mission School, and even more so at Livingstone High School. Lessons of nonracialism were also a major part of his upbringing. Before discussing that aspect of Dudley's life, we will review racism, oppression, and resistance between 1924 and 1940, the year he entered the University of Cape Town.

Racism and Resistance

Some of the people who taught Richard Dudley at Livingstone were beginning to become very politicized by the time Dudley graduated. There was resistance to racism and oppression throughout the country, including Cape Town, during his school years. Like the resistance that preceded Dudley's birth, organizations like the African National Congress, African Peoples' Organization, and other smaller groups were complex in that their members often contested radicalization and assimilation. This certainly continued to be the case in the African Peoples' Organization right up to Abdurahman's death in 1940. In his book *Twentieth Century South Africa*, William Beinart analyzes both oppression and resistance at the time:

> The 1920s and 1930s can be seen as a high point of segregation. Formal ideologies and policies were underpinned by widespread everyday racial prejudice in the language and behaviour of whites and sometimes others. Political accommodation in the rural areas, together with the difficulties of organization, stalled black national opposition. But state policy was by no means uncontested. There were alternative visions within the black and white populations. Moreover, at the very moment that segregation seemed entrenched, Smut's UP Cabinet (1939 to 1948) began to relax some of its elements. (Beinart, 994, p. 120)

The most powerful resistance in the 1920s came neither from the ANC nor APO but rather from the fledgling Industrial and Commercial Union (ICU), an organization that was founded in 1919 by Alfred Batty, a white Cape Town labor leader, and Clements Kadalie, a mission-educated Malawian who was the public leader of the organization. The ICU was initially more nonracial than the ANC and APO in that there were actually African, coloured, and white members. The union came of age through a 1919 strike on the docks in Cape Town and grew quickly as it was adaptable for workers and tenants throughout the country. A second major strike on the docks of Port Elisabeth ended with government violence, but the ICU grew to approximately 100,000 members by the late 1920s with locals in Zimbabwe and Malawi. In the early 1930s the union became mostly rural, and as quickly as Kadalie had built the organization it was dead. Depending on whom you read, the death of the ICU was due to government repression, populist fragmentation, infighting, and/or Kadalie's arrogance and corruption (Beinart, 1994, pp. 100–102; Thompson, 2000, p. 159).

The struggles of the ANC against both populist and government racism in the 1920s and 1930s continued to be fragmented by schisms between radicals and assimilationists. While there were demonstrations against discrimination and pass laws in Johannesburg, the organization in the Eastern Cape emphasized the vote and land. A Garveyite faction developed in what is now the Western Cape, and there was an alliance between the ANC and the Communist Party of South Africa (CPSA) after ANC president Josiah Gumede and CPSA representative James la Guma visited the Soviet Union together in 1927. The Gumede-Guma alliance created quite a rift in the Congress: the new radical guard versus the older voices of moderation. In 1930 the latter group won the ANC election, but both geographical and ideological schisms made the African National Congress irrelevant in the 1930s.

The government was also firm in the necessity of strengthening segregation, although in the late 1930s and 1940s there were both social and educational gaps. Between 1930 and 1932, Hertzog initiated the Native Economic Commission (NEC). The NEC report concluded that the problems of poor whites were directly related to Africans leaving the reserves and living in the cities. The report had the same tone as earlier liberal segregation and pointed out the importance of tribes, chiefs, and the rural preferences of African people. Just like the language of the turn of the twentieth century, the report had to make mention of the African's violent nature and blame the ruining of the land on the way Africans raise cattle. The culmination of the report was the passing of The Native Trust and Land Act and The Native Representation Act in 1936. Both laws, of course, offer a foreshadowing of the apartheid regime creating homelands for African people. While the legislation was referred to as "equitable segregation," Africans were no longer allowed to vote in the Cape (although it should be noted that the number of African voters was minimal) and the Government set up the Natives Representative Council (NRC) to represent Africans with white legislators. Because of harsh government repression in rural South Africa and the inner schisms of both the ANC and CPSA, neither organization provided much of an opposition voice at the time. However, The Native Trust and Land Act, The Native Representation Act, and other legislation in the Cape brought great concern to the coloured community.

In Dudley's early years, the APO was feeling pressure in the coloured community from both conservatives, who did not want to alienate whites and ruin the possibilities offered in Hertzog's promise of coloured preference, and radicals, who believed that the organization needed to serve the needs of the working class through trade unionism and activism. Abdurahman had often spoken in support of black trade unions, but when the organization decided to join the union game through its APO Federation of Labour Unions, the attempt was quite feeble. The escapade was pale in comparison with the ICU, and of course there were questions of why the APO would set up a union for coloureds rather than for all blacks, or for that matter all workers. It was also confusing because the APO supported the ICU, and Abdurahman spoke at ICU meetings. Typical of his position within the APO however, he made sure to warn workers of possible violent repercussions from whites. It did not take long for Kadalie and Abdurahman to oppose each other, but by then the APO foray into trade unionism was over just as the ICU would also be short-lived.

The general focus of the APO during the 1920s and into the 1930s was trying to find a way to fight the PACT government policies and legislation favoring white South Africans. They were not successful. Similar to its earlier life, the APO walked a fine line between fighting for a nonracial South Africa or simply representing the coloured elite. As we have already noted, the TLSA did not seem burdened by the same contradictions. The organization approved of the educational legislation in the early 1920s because they naively believed that coloured education would receive similar reforms and resources that had been afforded white schools. The League's political naivety is even more apparent in their belief that the Rand Revolt would benefit coloureds because the government would realize the brutality of the white working class. Articles in the *Education Journal* referred to the strikers as "Bolsheviks" in an attempt to distinguish themselves as "civilized." (Adhikari, 1993, p. 49)

Hertzog made promises of a New Deal for coloured South Africans that were to include economic opportunities and limited political rights.

> While he advocated total segregation for Africans, Coloureds (he declared) would be given political and economic, but not social equality with white Afrikaners, with whom they shared a language, history and undivided loyalty to South Africa. The Coloureds should have a distinct status apart from both the whites and the Africans. (Lewis, 1987, p. 124)

When the Nationalist Party was able to win the 1929 elections without the need of an alliance with the Labour Party, they no longer had to even make an appearance of promoting coloured rights. All of this just made the positions of the APO more confusing. While Abdurahman still made speeches promoting black unity, the organization changed the wording in the mission statement from "coloured races" to "coloured people" and admitted that they did not accept Africans in the organization. At the same time in the late 1920s and early 1930s, the TLSA continued to stress that it was not a political organization but rather an organization of professionals. While individual members of the League publicly stated their sadness at the poverty and the lack of jobs for coloured high school graduates—Stella Jacobs in her Masters thesis and Edward Roberts in his 1937 Presidential Address—the *Educational Journal* reaffirmed that the League's conservatism favored consultation and education, not adversarial politics, for the advancement of coloured people. They were soon to change to a policy of pedagogy and politics, but not quite yet.

In the late 1920s the APO was somewhat rejuvenated, but it was not because of successful campaigns, but rather further repressive legislation by the government. The creation of a Pension Act that guaranteed higher payoffs to whites, special certifications for coloured teachers, and a new coloured section in the Department of Education, as well as other discriminations buoyed the APO to public criticism. But to his credit, Abdurahman was able to get the APO to support the rights of Africans even though he was constantly reminded that there was a distinction between Africans and coloureds. He gave fiery speeches and warned his colleagues that discrimination against Africans would mean discrimination against themselves. "Let me warn you that once you admit that the coloured man has a right—no matter on what ground—to oust the native and take his job, then you cannot stop there. The European will then have a perfect right to ask for preferential treatment with respect for himself" (Lewis, 1987, p. 135). Of course white job preference was already the case, but within this context Abdurahman received the organization's authorization to work with other black organizations.

The ICU, ANC, and APO held a joint protest against the 1926 Colour Bar Bill, and Abdurahman organized joint conferences between 1927 and 1934. Representatives of the APO, ANC, ICU, South African Indian Council, Natal Indian Congress, Bantu Union, Cape Native Voters' Association, Griqua Union, and the CPSA attended the Non-European Conferences. Organizing these meetings was a great achievement for Abdurahman, and the conferences challenged government racism and oppression. All of the different organizations supported nonracist policies, but the meetings tended to return to moderation as a general stand. In the case of the APO, we have already noted that challenges had come from both conservatives and radicals. The most conservative coloured organization, the African National Bond (ANB), was formed in Cape Town in 1925 in cooperation with the Nationalist Party in the Cape. They asserted coloured superiority over Africans and trusted that a coalition with the Nationalist Party would bring both political and economic equality for coloured people. In fact, they referred to themselves as Eurafrican rather than coloured and put their faith in the white supremacy of the Nationalist Party. (Lewis, 1987, p. 143)

The radical challenge began to be felt from the sons and daughters of coloured leaders. Some like Cissie Gool, the daughter of Abdullah Abdurahman, Johnny Gomas, and James la Guma had joined the Communist Party; younger teachers in the Teachers' League of South Africa were beginning to challenge the moderation of the APO and the conservative policies and tone of the Teachers' League. There were similar radical voices in the ANC, ICU, and other organizations, but the conferences provided the old-guard black leadership with the critical mass needed to challenge the state while retaining their moderate ideologies. The tone of the conferences never stated demands but did condemn oppression and racism and asked for meetings with the government, which of course were turned down. While we might possibly make some connections between the conferences and the development of the Non-European Unity Movement (NEUM) and the rebirth of the ANC in the 1940s, it is probably best to say that the conferences became irrelevant as the various groups failed to come together, in spite of Abdurahman's efforts, to become a nonracial political organization. In addition, the government was able to pass further racist and repressive legislation.

The APO and the Conferences worked hard but accomplished little. The depression hurt the coloured community economically as did more laws that solidified segregation. As both Beinart and more recently Kallaway suggest, there were white liberals who opposed segregation, and there were attempts to address poverty in the coloured community through a coalition called the Coloured-European Councils. Although this was initially condemned by the APO as cooptation, Abdurahman later joined the conversation as a hope to challenge segregation and hold off the more radical coloured activists. The Coloured-European Councils consisted of white liberals and coloured leaders, and they addressed issues of social welfare, specifically growing poverty in the coloured community, without dealing with politics. The Councils were initially connected to the South African Institute of Race Relations (SAIRR), an organization founded in 1929 with the purpose of influencing Government through research and suggestion, not politics. SAIRR did a study on the economy of coloured South Africans in the early 1930s. Then the Coloured-European Councils, with support from coloured conservatives like Abe Desmore and George Golding, both members of the TLSA, and eventually the APO, convinced the government to commission a study on the economic conditions of coloured South Africans. The request came to Jan Hofmeyr, a member of the Fusion Government cabinet who appointed the Wilcocks Commission in 1934. Of the six members, Abdurahman was the only nonwhite, while two other people on the committee were viewed as liberals. The Commission was charged to study health, employment, housing, and education in the "Cape Coloured Community." They were to report on their findings without analysis or recommendations. Committee members, however, decided that recommendations were appropriate, but they had a difficult time coming to a consensus on most issues. The largest division within the committee was, on the one hand, finding solutions within the umbrella of the segregationist reality, and on the other hand, challenging the racialism that existed at the time and was a cause of coloured poverty. Conservative commissioners often blamed the victim regarding social welfare although they did agree that job, housing, and educational disparities needed to be addressed. Interestingly, the Commission did reference the plight of Africans, and even more surprisingly they reported on passing and coloured identity to emphasize the complexity of the construction of coloured in South Africa. So while the Commissioners agreed that recommendations had to come within the segregationist structure, Abdurahman and the liberal committee members dug in on two issues: the formation of a university for coloureds only and miscegenation laws. Abdurahman was greatly troubled when the Commission discussed separate social welfare and education departments for coloureds, a foreshadowing of more segregation in the years to follow.

The Wilcock Commission Report was published in 1938, and the Coloured-European Councils and the African Peoples' Organization held a conference to respond where delegates condemned the segregationist policies of the report. The government took no action regarding the report, and Lewis and others argue that it was simply a brief attempt to placate liberals and coloureds. The sociology department at the University of Cape Town did its own study in 1940, and that decade saw some liberal antisegregationist bills proposed in the South African senate. After the Wilcock Commission Report, the APO appeared to be even more irrelevant than before, as did the TLSA. It was in the context of segregationist policies and not very successful attempts at resistance that Richard Dudley learned nonracialism as a child and teenager.

Learning Nonracialism

In spite of the magnification of racism in South Africa during Richard Dudley's youth, as we noted at the outset his memories are of family, community, and school nonracialism. Dudley does, however, reflect on racialism in his life. Remember his earlier quote about his two younger sisters' occupational possibilities because they were "not so tan." Other examples included his cousin attending white schools and church racism during confirmation. We will discuss both events in this section. When Dudley speaks of his childhood in Newlands, there are many memories of a nonracial life both in his home and on the streets—something very different from other portrayals of childhood in 1920s South Africa. He has such an aversion to racial classifications that he still sees the need to sometimes use the phrase "so-called coloureds" or "so-called Jews" or "so-called blacks" or "so-called whites" and so on. When he refers to his "draught board" family, with black people and white people, he does not appear to make judgments or distinctions. Yet because of racialism in South Africa, it is certainly relevant that his sisters and uncle qualified for certain jobs because of the color of their skin and that his cousin who lived on the other side of their two-family house attended schools that were designated white. Remember we are still talking about the 1920s and 1930s before the apartheid era.

> In those days it was not an uncommon thing for people who were sufficiently untanned to be classified as white. And so this aunt of mine who had a built-in tan of some measure married somebody whose tan was I think not very evident, and he worked in the local brewery. He was one of the senior people in the dispatch section. And their son, who is light in colour, although we lived next door, I went to St. Andrews Anglican Mission School, but they were able to send him to a primary school in the next street, Dean Street Primary School. When he had finished his primary school he went to Rondebosch Boys School. So we lived next door to each other and we used to help each other—me at Livingstone and he at Rondebosch Boys High School. (Dudley Interview, 2002)

While Dudley's family and other South Africans transcended and transgressed racism, it must be clearly stated that issues of racial designation, and later passing, divide and hurt people; and in South Africa, especially under apartheid laws, destroyed many families—part of the evil of pigmentocracy.

Memories of the time in Dudley's neighborhood in Newlands exhibit people living and working together. Dudley remembers people from varying backgrounds living on the street—British, Italian, coloured, German, and others. People from different races and religions came to the street to sell produce and meats. In addition, the home of Samuel and Alleta Dudley attracted visitors, and racial or religious designations did not appear to determine who visited.

> I realized that somebody was a Muslim or somebody was a Hindu, but it did not matter because the reason they came to our house was a human one. Our house was a meeting place for quite a large number of people at different times. And again it was what one might call in modern terms nonracial in that you had people of different colors and different social classes visiting there. During that time there were lots of people of all colors who were out of work. And in one way or another they were associated with my father in his providing support systems for them. (Dudley Interview, 2001)

Dudley recalls his father helping people, especially Indians, fill out job applications. They came to him because he was a schoolmaster. His father also hired handymen who often were white. A final example from home adds to the complexity, because the context is of Aunt Maude teaching in a white school in Mafekeng in the northern part of the Cape. Maude had taught at a mission school in Cape Town as well as Trafalgar before she took the post in Mafekeng. Dudley's reflections on her move are interesting but only because they confound issues of race: "The other strange thing I would say is that my aunt taught in Mafekeng at a so-called white school. Because a lot of people there in that particular area of course acquired the kind of tan with which my aunt was born, and she was able to teach at a white school" (Dudley Interview, 2002). His aunt became friends with the mayor's family, whose daughters she taught, and who were Jewish with the name of Rosenberg.

> And during the course of the Christmas holidays these two girls used to come along and spend the holidays with my aunt at our home. I remember the older one's name was Sonia. I used to play along with my sisters. We did not see these girls as being very special. They were Jewish girls, but we just did not see them as such, not that I can remember. Because they used to play in the river and so on, go for walks with them all over the place. And this used to happen over quite a period of time, even right up to the time that my aunt retired there. So that fit into our lives something which I think was quite significant in that it would not happen today. (Dudley Interview, 2002)

Dudley's memories of St. Andrews Mission School are also of a diverse population without discrimination, and he concludes that his childhood included "white and black and speckled. I think as far as my own upbringing was concerned, I cannot actually say with any kind of confidence that we grew up with any kind of feeling of being discriminated against."

Lessons of nonracialism continued at Livingstone, but there was a definite racial incident involving Dudley and his brother at church.

> Out of courtesy to my parents, when I was sixteen, I did present myself to the Anglican Church for confirmation. That's the time I got that Bible from my parents. I used to attend the lessons in the evening at St. Andrew's Church. So, we presented ourselves in church on the day on which we were going to be confirmed. I didn't take notice of who was in the confirmation class. It was my brother and I, and when we presented ourselves in church, we found that two groups of candidates were being presented. One was tan and the others were not so tan. Yes, and were confirmed in separate groups. Yes, and that was the last time I ever attended church. (Dudley Interview, 2002)

At Livingstone Dudley and fellow students were made aware of racism in society, but they were also pushed academically and urged toward success. The teaching of nonracialism was not as overt as it was when Dudley became a teacher and he and his colleagues stressed the fallacies of race in the 1940s and during apartheid. But the makeup of the faculty was multiracial. "We had that unusual state of affairs where you had three nonwhite women who had actually graduated at the University. The school at the time had a

United Nations staff. Mr. Roberts was the principal, but you had quite a number of other people there who would have been classified as white." While the school was founded as a high school to serve the coloured community, there were Africans who attended Livingstone when Dudley was in high school. For example, he recalls discussions on socialism and imperialism with Israel Kobus, the younger brother of a founding member of NEUM, Cadoc Kobus, who had come to attend Livingstone from the Transkei. As a matter of information, Dudley recalls that the discussions were beyond him and other students, but that would change in the not too distant future. What he was aware of at the time was that teachers like Fataar and Grammer were amongst a growing number of educators who were highly critical of the government and the soon to come Coloured Affairs Department. Dudley concluded his discussions about his student days at Livingstone, however, with a note on nonracialism:

> I don't think I would have taken notice of the fact that Miss Douglas and Miss Ruskin were Jewish. Cairns, despite his name, was Afrikaner. We knew that Jooste was an Afrikaner and so on. But he wasn't a white Afrikaner. To us he was a damn good Afrikaans teacher. There was Miss Ward. She was a highly civilized, helpful person, and we didn't think of her, I don't think man, I'm telling you quite honestly I didn't think of those people in terms of color. (Dudley Interview, 2002)

Conclusions

Despite being born at a time when the South African government was legislating more and more segregationist policy to the delight of many of the country's white citizens, Richard Dudley was raised in a family, community, and schools that nurtured both a love of learning and nonracialism. This type of upbringing and schooling was not the reality for great numbers of his black contemporaries. Examples abound in the auto/biographical literature of racism and discrimination. Dudley, of course, would learn the realities of racism in South Africa not long after he finished his schooling at Livingstone. Richard Dudley's love of education and his unbending belief in nonracialism began as a child and teen; his family, community, and schools were influential. Education and nonracialism continued to be important, and he began his political life as well when he entered the University of Cape Town in 1940.

3

education and politics

Lessons for Teaching and Struggle

Richard Dudley enrolled in the University of Cape Town as a fifteen-year-old just three months after Great Britain declared war on Germany. The war caused a huge rift in the ruling United Party, and Hertzog left the party as the country joined the allied war effort in eastern Africa, northern Africa, and Italy. While Dudley became interested in the war through his teachers at Livingstone, he entered UCT as a very focused and serious student. Although he wanted to study history and English, he had agreed to the "request" of the elders at Livingstone to study science and math. He came to the University with an excellent academic background and was committed to success at UCT. So much so that he informed his future wife, Iris Atkins, that he would not be able to spend much time with her during his first year, because all of his hours would be taken with his studies. However, the unofficial political teachings of some of his teachers at Livingstone, Tippy Davids in particular, and the knowledge of the antiracist political work of Allie Fataar and others had rubbed off, and academic studies were joined by politics during Dudley's years at the University. Besides the sciences, Dudley studied history and he was influenced by professors at the University as well as somewhat older members of the New Era Fellowship (NEF), a fledgling political organization that had weekly meetings where members discussed South Africa within the context of anti-imperialism and nonracialism. It was in the Fellowship that Dudley began his political awakening in 1941.

University of Cape Town

The University of Cape Town was a segregated institution when Dudley enrolled in 1940. Because South Africa was involved in World War II, a handful of black students were allowed to enroll as the University had determined that it was too difficult for students to travel to Europe and India for their studies. Dudley's memories of UCT include his academic studies and race. He spent his first two years taking courses in mathematics and science—chemistry and physics in particular. His courses were rigorous and he was highly successful. While many students in his classes did not welcome him and other students of color into their group, there were others whom he worked with in his laboratories and classes.

> There was very little association between so-called white students in the classes and the so-called nonwhite students. I didn't detect in the classes that I attended any kind of racism on the part of the tutors. But I think that there seemed to be a certain amount of standoffishness amongst the white students. Not that we wanted actually to obtrude upon their presence one way or another. (Dudley Interview, 2002)

There were students that Dudley worked with as he completed the first two years of his studies. He had a lab partner who was an Afrikaner and an English-speaking classmate whom he studied with who later became a classics professor at Rhodes University. In a number of cases he earned the top grade in his science courses and received the class award for his work. On one such occasion there was a reaction that Dudley interestingly refers to as "just one thing, a tiny thing yes."

> When the results came out my name was right at the top. They wanted to know who this individual is because I would not have been known by name to the majority of the people in the class there, except the so-called darkies. I don't know whether that produced envy or respect. But then in the next examination I got 100 percent along with a few others, so I remained there in the top group. And then at the end of the year I was awarded the medal in the physics class. Certain of the white students went to complain to the professor, doubting whether I had been good enough to earn that medal. (Dudley Interview, 2002)

Richard Dudley also worked closely with a number of professors at the University. He remembers them all, and most of those memories are of teachers who were both civil and helpful. When he finished his first two years of math and science classes, he began preparation in teacher education and work on his masters degree in biology. Both were completed within a five-year university career. One of his fellow students in the teacher preparation program was Tom Hanmer, who was to become his lifelong comrade in the Teachers' League of South Africa. They took all of their course work together, and Dudley remembers specifics from many of the courses. He recalls the encouragement of professors and that most of them treated both Tom Hanmer and himself as young adults as they were doing their teacher training curriculum. They took methods courses, psychology courses, and courses in the history and philosophy of education. The lecturer in the history of South African education was the well-known historian Edward Pells. Seven decades after the course, Dudley reflected after he did further reading on the topic:

> A very matter-of-fact sort of individual, a Rhodes scholar as well. But I also think that the history of South African education that he taught us was somewhat deficient. I didn't know it then, I got to know it as I did reading on my own, and later on as I did reading for the articles I wrote for the *Educational Journal*. Because I don't think that he saw that the education of nonwhites in this country was an instrument of government, instrument of ruling South Africa. While his lectures were delivered in a very nice way, I think there was a little bit of shallowness. (Dudley Interview, 2002)

They also took philosophy of education, where there was emphasis on a system of pedagogy that presented whites as moral and superior. Dudley recalls that the professor was very leery of both himself and Hanmer because he associated their high schools, Livingstone and Trafalgar, as political. Or was this also a sign of covert racism? The implications, of course, of Pells teaching the South African commonplace history and philosophy of education stressing white superiority, are at least covertly racist by definition. Curriculum as overt racism, however, existed not just during the apartheid era but also at the time Dudley was at University. Zachariah Matthews reflected on his history course at Fort Hare University, the first university for Africans in the country. He was a student in 1940.

> Our history, as we had absorbed it from the tales and talk of our elders, bore no resemblance to South African history as it has been written by European scholars, or as it is taught in South African schools, and as it was taught to us at Fort Hare. . . . We struggled through the white man's version of the so-called Kaffir Wars, the Great Trek, the struggles for control of South Africa. . . . And we had to give back in our examination papers the answers the white man expected. (Matthews, 1989, pp. 58, 59)

Dudley describes one other event as somewhat racial during his studies at the University. As part of his teacher training he took a language course, and the professor assigned various readings that would be discussed in class through presentations. One particular reading was a play that subtly showed the likeness of Adolf Hitler and D. F. Malan. The same instructor asked Hanmer and Dudley to report on a pamphlet by Booker T. Washington. When they responded to the selection critically, the teacher stopped taking them as students.

While Richard Dudley did not remember racism being a prominent part of his education at the University of Cape Town, Tom Hanmer, who was a UCT student at the same time, has different memories:

> UCT was "open" very much in inverted commas. During the time that I was there, I could belong to any of the academic societies. So, for example, a drama society, I didn't ever do that, music society. But not any of the sports clubs, couldn't make use of any of the sports facilities, so we couldn't play rugby or soccer or make use of the swimming pool or play tennis. Several friends of mine were doing medicine. When they did their practical work, whenever a white patient was examined by the professor or lecturer as a demonstration to the class, they had to leave. They couldn't even work on a white cadaver. (Hanmer Interview, 1999)

Helen Kies enrolled in the University a few years after Dudley and Hanmer, and her recollections of racism are also quite strong:

> Then I went to UCT. It was racist—very, very racist. You felt totally out of place as far as both the lecturers and your fellow white students were concerned. They'd just exclude you completely. There was a math lecturer whom I had to ask for advice every now and then. He'd just ignore me. He wouldn't answer any of my questions. I decided I was there for a purpose and would get on with the job. I wouldn't allow their behavior to bother me. I attended lectures, did my work. (Kies Interview, 1999)

Dudley does question himself about whether or not his academic successes mitigated overt racism, but Hanmer and Kies were also outstanding students, and they clearly remember UCT as a racist institution. The declarations of racism certainly would not be dismissed by Dudley, and it might be that reactions to racism at the institution, and the general racism in South African society at the time, are similar in content but not in tone.

Learning Politics

As we have noted above, the political education of Richard Dudley began when he was a student at the University. There is some irony in that fact because there were actually quiet government calls for easing segregation during Dudley's years at UCT. The reasons are unclear but possibly include black resistance, the work of South African Institute of Race Relations and other white liberal university research, or the realization of the need for black skilled labor in the modern, capitalist, industrial world. We must be clear that Smuts and others in his government were not advocating racial equality or social integration. However, some ministers such as Jan Hofmeyr, who we met in the last chapter in relation to the Wilcock Commission, challenged different aspects of racism throughout their lives in government. Hofmeyr held various cabinet positions and in the 1930s and 1940s questioned ethnic and racial commonplaces. Hofmeyr made the following pronouncement in Parliament. "I take my stand on the ultimate removal of the colour bar from our constitution" (Thompson, 2000, p. 180). While Hofmeyr's views on the color bar were not always consistent, he made statements and used language that was certainly not the norm for his peers, especially fellow Afrikaner politicians (Paton, 1964). However, liberalism did exist throughout the WWII years. Peter Kallaway's recent article, "Welfare and Education in British Colonial Africa and South Africa during the 1930s and 1940s," presents some examples. Kallaway emphasizes liberal, economic capitalism but does not vilify South African politicians who spoke against segregation as pawns of industrial capitalism. For example, he analyzes the changes in Edgar Brookes, a white representative for blacks in the Natives Representative Council, regarding race and education:

> In the later book he was concerned to emphasize that any attempt to frame a policy in this field that treated blacks as having distinct needs fell short on political and economic grounds. Whites would only punish themselves in the long run if they deprived their fellow citizens of education or tried to promote a separate form of education for them, as this would not only be blatantly unjust in the emerging context of international politics but would prove to be politically and economically "irrational" in the context of the emerging economy. (Kallaway, 2005, p. 351)

In a similar vein, the Social and Economic Planning Council report on social welfare argued for adequate educational facilities and free primary education for all blacks by 1960, and the United Party floated a plan for a common curriculum for blacks and whites in urban areas. Finally, as the war ended Hofmeyr initiated a school-feeding program for both white and black children who were poor. Of course all of these small attempts at reform through the United Party were stillborn when the Nationalist Party won the 1948 election, and the apartheid era began. Dudley and his comrades in the New Era Fellowship would not participate in such liberal reforms that they viewed, of course, as collaborationist.

The foundation of political organizations that Dudley affiliated with in the 1940s, including the New Era Fellowship, Non-European Unity Movement, and the Teachers' League of South Africa, began with the Trotskyist movement gaining a South African voice around 1935. Leon Trotsky was deported from the Soviet Union in 1929 as a threat to Stalin's power. Ideologically the split was between Stalin's program of socialism in the Soviet Union and Trotsky's theory of worldwide permanent revolution. In South Africa the Communist Party purged some members in the early 1930s, and there was a move to a loose grouping of socialists who supported the teachings of Trotsky. They planned to form a nonracial working class party, but the goal never became the reality. Like the ANC in the 1920s and 1930s, there were ideological schisms and also geographical divisions, with urban groups focusing on workers and rural groups emphasizing peasants. In addition, there was a divide between Johannesburg and Cape Town.

The Lenin Club began in the early 1930s in Cape Town. Originally Yiddish speaking, it quickly became a Trotskyist nonracial discussion group that included many of the people who Dudley joined as a comrade in the 1940s. Members included Goolam Gool, Jane Gool, Saul Jayiya, and Isaac Tabata, all future leaders in the Non-European Unity Movement. The Lenin Club organized various activities and events, including a socialist Sunday school for children, study groups, and a number of public political meetings. Unfortunately, like the political organizations on the left that preceded and followed, the Lenin Club had ideological and personality splits that caused it to fade into other political organizations like the Communist League of South Africa (CLSA) and the Workers' Party.

One further schism that included Dudley's future comrades centers around the National Liberation League (NLL), an organization that was formed in 1935. Although the NLL attempted to be a national organization, most of the membership was in Cape Town and included many young coloured people who were the sons and daughter of the coloured elite. The organization initially stood opposite the African Peoples' Organization and proposed protests, marches, and working class unity. Johnny La Guma composed the NLL anthem that was sung at meetings:

> Dark folk, arise! The long, long night is over;
> Faint in the east, Behold the dawn appear:
> Out of your evil dream of toil and sorrow,
> Arise, ye dark folk, For the dawn is here! (Abrahams, 1954, p. 326)

The NLL firmly stood for noncollaboration with segregated institutions. Lewis concisely defines the loosely formed organization that included communists, Trotskyists, and other socialists.

> The solutions they adopted included, broadly speaking, rejection of a narrow Coloured identity in favour of a broader black and working-class alliance, and the adoption of mass action in the form of strikes, demonstrations and boycotts, to achieve their goals of complete equality for all races in a non-racial and democratic South Africa. (Lewis, 1987, p. 180)

The two factions that emerged in the NLL were both led by members of the Gool family. Cissie Gool, who as we have already noted was the daughter of Abdullah Abdurahman, led a group that we might refer to as the more activist faction. Cissie Gool's brother-in-law, Goolam Gool, was the leader of the second group, a faction that might be referred to as more academic and purist. It was the second faction that Dudley would become part of in NEF, NEUM, and the TLSA. It should be mentioned, however, that often individuals crossed over on specific issues. Both factions interpreted issues from a socialist perspective and viewed the inequality and racism in South Africa through a lens of British and South African imperialism and capitalism. Each side had a vision of a union of blacks and whites defeating the enemy in South Africa and throughout the world—Trotsky's permanent revolution.

The break, however, was over activism and noncollaboration. The faction that Cissie Gool led had ties to whites in the Communist Party, of which she was a member, and believed that the organization needed to be involved in local politics. Cissie Gool worked closely with Sam Kahn, who was a white communist and member of the Cape Town City Council. She followed her father onto the Cape Town City Council in 1938 when she was elected from the Woodstock section of the city. With other members as well as people from the CPSA, she provided testimony to the Wilcocks Commission. Pragmatism was more important to her than ideology, and the Goolam Gool faction viewed the activism as collaboration. That said, both groups worked together against the Struttaford Servitude Acts in the late 1930s, the law that foreshadowed apartheid forced removals. Together and even with help of the African Peoples' Organization, they organized a National Protest Day in 1939 against the Acts. 15,000 people attended in Cape Town.

Goolam Gool's group believed strongly in noncollaboration and included future leaders of NEUM and the TLSA, Isaac Tabata and Ben Kies. They argued against participation in government organizations like the Natives Representative Council and the Cape Town City Council. They also strongly believed that it was wrong to participate in the political party system, pointing out the collaborationism of the African Peoples' Organization, because the parties were all servants of capitalism. Finally, they strongly condemned "colouredism" or what some people called "Abdurahmanism" as they argued for full equality for all people. The position on full equality would soon be seen in the Ten Point Programme of the Non-European Unity Movement.

There were ebbs and flows in who controlled the National Liberation League, but it folded soon after the National Day of Protest. The Goolam Gool, Tabata, and Kies branch started the New Era Fellowship in 1937, and four years later the organization would become central to the political education of Richard Dudley. The New Era Fellowship was founded as a sophisticated socialist debate society where issues of imperialism and capitalism were connected to inequality and racism in South Africa. Goolam Gool was chairman, Ben Kies vice chairman, Hawa Ahmed secretary, and Salie Edross, the man who recruited Richard Dudley to the organization, was organizing secretary. We have already noted the many schisms in and across leftist organizations in South Africa, and of course they remain to this day. However, political and personal commemorations like *More than Brothers*, Hein Willemse's collection on Cape Town artist Peter Clarke and writer James Matthews, and Shamil Jeppie and Crain Soudien's *The Struggle for District Six*, a late apartheid conference and publication for the Hands Off District Six Committee, portray the life, intellect, and breadth of the New Era Fellowship. In the latter collection, Dudley honors the fellowship.

> When one traces the development of political organizations through the National Liberation League, the Non-European Front, the Anti-CAD Movement, the All-African Convention, the Unity Movement and Congress organizations which operated in the Western Cape, one sees the origins of the basic conceptions of a *national* solution for all South Africa and the structures and ideas upon which a truly *national liberatory movement came to be based*. . . . The New Era Fellowship, established in 1937, was to become the single most influential training ground for students and workers in those early years. In fact, the Stakesby-Lewis Hostel in Canterbury Street was the centre of some of the most fruitful developments in the new ideology that was to sweep South Africa after the second world war. The Hostel deserves a special place in the history of the District. It was here, for example, that the National Anti-CAD movement was launched in 1943. (Dudley, 1990, p. 200)

The New Era Fellowship met for over twenty years at the Stakesby Lewis Hostel in District Six. Speakers included people like Dora Taylor who worked closely with Tabata and was the author of *The Role of the Missionaries*, Eddie Roux, who wrote *Time Longer than Rope*, and Peter Abrahams, whose book *Tell Freedom*, includes a portrait of Goolam Gool. Abrahams stayed with Gool when he first arrived in Cape Town from Johannesburg and he came to admire Gool, who he was also especially grateful to for the kindness

Goolam Gool's family showed him when he arrived in the city. However, he decided that he needed to move on from the Gool household after a meeting of the New Era Fellowship. Abrahams addressed the Fellowship on the topic of non-European literature in South Africa, and there were both communists and Trotskyists in the audience. During the question section Abrahams sided with the communist, Johnny Gomas, rather than Gool, and he knew that Gool was both upset and hurt. In *Tell Freedom* he addresses left schisms as well as his view of Goolam Gool.

> Yet both Gool and Gomas were bitterly opposed to racialism, and both were sincere and honest in their strivings for non-European emancipation. And each was all that was untrustworthy to the other. Labels had conquered the men. . . . I wanted to convey to him (Gool) before I left. And I wanted to say to him: Of all the Coloureds I've met, you are, most completely, most naturally, free of the slightest hint of prejudice, upwards, to whites, or downwards, to the blacks. (Abrahams, 1954, pp. 328, 329)

The New Era Fellowship viewed itself as both highly academic and political, and the general theme was solidarity of all oppressed non-Europeans throughout the world, not just in South Africa. Dudley described his first individual presentation; Ben Kies was the respondent.

> My second year in the study group I was given the chance to speak to the study group. My task was to examine the position of native labour in South Africa. Now we used to sit in a horseshoe shape, you see. And the person who was due to speak would be in the center so that you faced everybody there. And so you go along there full of yourself and full of this information and so on. You feel that you've done a good job. And then the tutors start taking you apart. You go in there and you think that you're Gulliver in Lilliput. You shrink in size but you learn an important lesson, and that is analysis. (Dudley Interview, 1999)

Dudley acknowledged that Ben Kies could be difficult but he greatly admired and respected both his politics and intellect. Dudley's caveat is that Kies had "arms not wings."

> Ben Kies was an extremely well-read person. Some people regarded him as being very, shall I say, somewhat bullying. But, I don't think that that was true. I think that Ben Kies read a great deal across a very wide spectrum. Although he had done his major degree in English literature, he was one who chose to read the literature of all the continents and he introduced us to a kind of bibliography that

> we ourselves would not have been able to arrive at unless we had gone through the same process. I would say he didn't have that sort of bullying nature. He had a very persuasive nature. (Dudley Interview, 2005)

While Dudley was focused on his academic work as a fifteen-year-old first-year university student, he did meet a fellow student who was a member of the NEF. He had been warned by the Livingstone school committee to stay away from politics. The school committee used the New Era Fellowship as an example. Dudley met both Ben Kies and Salie Edross at the University, and as organizing secretary it was Edross's job to recruit members. In fact, he recruited students from both Trafalgar and Livingstone. Dudley began going to NEF meetings, and more politically astute members provided reading lists that corresponded to the organization's analysis and critique of capitalism, imperialism, inequality, and racism. At the University students were allowed to check out four library books at one time, and Dudley used half of his allotment for the sciences and half for politics and history. He began reading texts like Burnhall and Engels. He read Voltaire's *Candide*. He also read the vast amount of work that was being published by Victor Gollananz's Left Book Club, and he dove into the critical utopian work of Robert Owen. He still reads Owen today.

During his first year in the NEF, Dudley read and attended meetings, and the second year he was sponsored as being serious about politics by an older member, so he began to attend specific study groups. Meetings were held on Sunday mornings and included speakers and discussions. Dudley remembers addresses by Goolam Gool, Jane Gool, Issac Tabata, and Saul Jayiya. Allie Fataar would speak on *Das Kapital* and analyze capitalism and profit. There were discussions of historical materialism and particularly memorable is a lesson learned one Sunday morning in 1943 from Ben Kies.

> Ben Kies walked in with a copy of a newspaper called *The Sun*. There was an announcement that the government was going to set up a special commission to deal with the affairs of the coloured people. He gave us this article and then asked us what we felt about it. We made comments, I suppose, which were inconsequential, and then he pointed out the significance of this for us. Now that showed me that if you don't have a system of analysis you can actually read a newspaper and miss completely the actual importance. And, well, from that point on, I would say that I don't really know how many stages there were of being made politically conscious, but that was one of the things that I'll never forget that made me leap into this kind of action in understanding things and then deciding what needed to be done, because we were drawn into the opposition to this at the time. (Dudley Interview, 2003)

Besides general reading and analysis, Dudley sometimes lectured at meetings during his second year, and he would prepare extensively when he led study groups that were also often held on Sundays. He reflected on how he and others in the NEF prepared for organization meetings and study groups:

> In the study circles there was a structured process of teaching people historical analysis. I think that we went through the ways in which history was approached, not merely by the well-known academic, classical Marxists, but we went through the approaches of the seventeenth century English writers, the eighteenth century. And we went through, for example, the works of Hobbes, *The Leviathan*. And then we went on to learn about the teachings of the Hegelians and then Marx. (Dudley Interview, 2003)

Members of the organization published in a magazine called *Trek* that was similar to the *New Statesman* in England, a left wing publication. Dora Taylor, for example, did book reviews, and Eddie Roux was a frequent contributor. The magazine addressed issues of racialism and more specifically coloured leadership and politics. Perfect topics considering the New Era Fellowship saw itself as nonracial and opposed all racialism including that of the coloured elite exemplified in the African Peoples' Organization.

Dudley's involvement in the NEF was ironically in opposition to the old guard Teachers' League that his father had given up on years earlier. However, neither his father nor his mother thought of his Fellowship mentors as "being exactly sponsors of my welfare. My mother was concerned by this sort of thing because of the fact of my youth. She always wondered whether I was going to be picked up just as a passenger somewhere along the way." Many years later Alleta Dudley did have to endure the questions of authorities regarding her son. She of course denied any knowledge of his whereabouts.

Dudley continued his political reading and also became involved with the Student Socialist Society at UCT. He scanned the stalls on the Parade in the central business district in Cape Town for political books, and he became a constant visitor at Paul Kosten's Modern Books, a leftist bookstore in the city. Kosten was an American expatriate socialist who was involved in left-wing politics in Cape Town, and he was a friend of Ben Kies. The bookstore had a policy of allowing students to linger and browse, and there was good conversation as well as anticapitalist and anti-imperialist literature. In 1945 Kosten began advertising in the *Educational Journal*: "We offer an intelligent service to those who use books." At the University Dudley met with students in the Student Socialist Movement and often used his education at the New Era Fellowship in these meetings. In addition, there was a strong right-wing movement on campus—Brown shirts—who held pro-German rallies. Dudley's campus political involvement introduced him to his future comrade, Hosea Jaffe, the author of *Three Hundred Years*. He met professors who were socialists and he continued to hone his political analysis studying Hegel and Marx. Just before Dudley graduated from UCT, he and a number of the younger members of the New Era Fellowship, including Helen Kies, took more of a leadership role because their "elders" were busy with their involvement with other political organizations—the Non-European Unity Movement and the transformed Teachers' League of South Africa. Dudley, Kies, and their young comrades recruited students to the organization from the University, teacher training colleges, and high schools. They set up a student organization called the Non-European Students' Association to prepare new members for entry into the NEF, but they also began their work in the other organizations passing out pamphlets for meetings and events in opposition to the rising Coloured Affairs Department.

Dudley graduated from the University of Cape Town in 1944 with a bachelor's degree, master's degree, and teacher certification. He did teaching practice during his final university year at Livingstone High School, and he was destined to return there as a teacher the following year, the first of thirty-nine years. In some ways he also graduated with an undergraduate degree in anticapitalist, antiimperialist, and antiracist politics from the New Era Fellowship. As he began his long career in teaching in 1945, he also started his life-long career in politics through multiple fellowships, NEUM, and the TLSA.

4

becoming a teacher, becoming a comrade

Pre-Apartheid Years

As Richard Dudley was completing his studies at the University of Cape Town, he was also becoming more involved in politics through the New Era Fellowship. He flirted with furthering his graduate studies, but there were still two younger sisters and his relationship with Iris Atkins was becoming more serious, so family responsibilities led him to accept a position as a teacher at his alma mater, Livingstone High School. The early and mid-1940s, in spite of some attempts at liberal reforms, were becoming even more racist. The United Party feared losing white votes to the overt racism of the Nationalist Party and responded with additional government segregation policies. The Natives Representative Council became more entrenched as the United Party continued to make divide-and-rule policies to partition black South Africans. Segregationist policies, however, were met with changes in black resistance. The African National Congress came back on the scene after a quiet period in the late 1930s, and there were new attempts, beyond the National Liberation League, at nonracial organized resistance. Dudley became more politically involved as he assumed leadership roles in both the Unity Movement and Teachers' League.

Before tracing Dudley's teaching and politics through the years that preceded the election of the Nationalist Party in 1948, it is important to briefly describe the work of the African National Congress in the 1940s. Although Dudley never had any affiliation with the ANC, it is the only viable South African political party at the present time, and its rebirth began in the decade before apartheid. Dormant in the late 1930s, the organization began to rebuild membership when it elected American- and British-trained physician Alfred Xuma as president in 1940. Because Smuts had eased pass laws, there were a growing number of Africans moving to South African cities, and with them came the migration issues of poverty and resistance. In Cape Town the multiple issues of social welfare, unemployment, and education were magnified as more and more Africans came to settle in the Langa community that was started in 1927 (Bickford-Smith, van Heyningen, Worden, 1999, pp. 87–91). In Johannesburg both Soweto and Alexandra were growing each day. The ANC spoke out regarding discrimination, but the organization was conflicted, just as it had been in the 1930s. For example, in 1943 the ANC published *African Claims* and demanded equal rights for all people. At the same time, however, they were relatively quiet when people in the Alexandra Township boycotted buses because of high fares, when squatters occupied land in Soweto chanting Sofasonke (We Shall Die), and when the African Mineworkers' Union struck in 1946.

In the mid-1940s the beginning of a radicalized ANC was starting to form within the newly created ANC-Youth League that included future leaders like Nelson Mandela and Walter Sissulu. Until 1947 the president of the Youth League was Anton Lembede, who was ironically a young lawyer in the office of former ANC president, Pixley Seme. Lembede did not have any of Seme's conservatism, but rather brought many of the ideas of Marcus Garvey to the Youth League as he argued for African self-reliance. Lembede died suddenly in 1947, and the Youth League was left to the more left-wing, activist, and nonracial alliance of Mandela, Sissulu, Tambo, and others that won leadership of the ANC in 1949 as the apartheid era began.

Becoming a Teacher

Dudley and his comrades had great ideological differences with the ANC as the years went on. Although he was politically active in 1945, Dudley's major concern was being a first-year teacher. He was twenty when he began teaching, and one of his first issues was that students in the school, especially senior girls, were very close to his age, and many of them were not particularly interested in their lessons. Dudley spoke of initial awkwardness because he had to learn how to be a "schoolmaster type" even though he was very young. Fortunately he had mentors, as both the principal and other teachers were encouraging and provided pedagogical and academic leadership. Dudley also used his classes at UCT with Professor Grant as a model, and he was not satisfied with rote learning. "It certainly wasn't easy, I would say, because you could easily adopt a sort of lecture approach, you know, as if you were sort of simply pouring ladles and ladles into these plates that you assume exist in their heads" (Dudley Interview, 2003). Grant used a question-and-answer approach, called "inquiry" today, and in the beginning Dudley saw his job as pulling out what his students knew and taking them further.

> There were certain things that were obvious to those pupils because they had done it before. But now you had to use their grasp of this to get their particular bite in the lessons that you were teaching. It's a question of making the familiar so simple that you could talk to them and assume that they knew what you were talking about. Then you had to latch on to the new things that you were doing. We were also at that stage, I think, taught to adapt things in the lessons in a practical way, and to get them to participate in demonstrating and so on. (Dudley Interview, 2003)

Dudley's first mentor as a teacher at Livingstone was Edward Maurice's brother, George Maurice, but he left the staff the following year to pursue a medical degree at the University of Cape Town. Initially Dudley taught math, science, and English, but he gave up English the next year when Maurice left the faculty. His pedagogical memories from the first year are of teaching English, and his former teachers at Livingstone served as the model as he had students read aloud and perform the books they studied. During his early years at the school he also taught Latin, and his memories are of good students who were serious about the language. He was pressed into teaching Latin, for just a short time because the subject was being phased out at the school, and he was also able to drop math when George Abrahams moved from the lower school to the senior high school after he qualified as a senior teacher. Even then Livingstone, unlike some schools, was very concerned with credentials, and Roberts, as the principal, enforced standards.

For Dudley and others at the school at the time, such as Roberts, Fataar, Grammer, high standards were a political issue. Dudley remembers that even before the apartheid regime took over in 1948, different curriculums for white and coloured schools meant that certain laboratory practicums and experiments were taken out of the science curriculum for coloured schools. Differentiated curriculum became an important issue for Dudley and his Teachers' League comrades during apartheid, but even in the 1940s he developed his own curriculum that contradicted the "coloured curriculum." There were also issues of creating possibilities for students who were not academic. Remember that legislation had limited construction apprenticeships for black South Africans with the 1921 Juveniles Act and the 1922 Apprenticeship Act. Dudley and his colleagues at Livingstone worked around the syllabus in the 1940s with practical math and science to prepare some Livingstone students for the apprenticeship exams and future employment. This is an interesting issue that we will return to, because much of the educational criticism directed at teachers like Dudley who affiliated with NEUM was that they favored the academically talented and ignored those students who were not as intelligent. Because of the TLSA and NEUM presence at the school, nonracialism and noncollaboration were part of both the tone and teaching of Livingstone High School.

Dudley speaks with fond recollections of two white teachers, Hendrik Esterhuzien the art teacher and Charles Humphries the woodwork teacher, as he discusses nonracial teaching in the 1940s. Esterhuzien taught at the school for many years, and quite amazingly two well-known artists were his students in the 1940s. Peter Clarke still lives in Cape Town, but his paintings have been exhibited throughout the world, and although he was only a student at Livingstone for one year, he has great appreciation for Esterhuzien and the school. He refers to Livingstone as a "school of the mind" in spite of the fact that he is quick to acknowledge that he was not an academic student. Albert Adams graduated from Livingstone in the 1940s, and he too recalls that he was not much of a student. He has lived in London for many years and was an instructor at Slade School of Art. He credits Esterhuzien and Frank Grammer for changing his life.

> Well I think certainly, had I not gone to Livingstone, my life would have been totally different and different in the way that probably I wouldn't have had the kinds of experiences, obviously, that I have subsequently had. I most probably would have ended up having left school at Standard Eight and done any kind of job that would have brought in a salary. I don't know, but looking at my contemporaries who had been at school with me and left early, my uncles and aunts. They ended up by marrying early, by having children early, having really a very difficult life. I was able to live my own life the way I wanted to live it. I don't think I would have been able to had it not been for the fact that I continued the education at Livingstone. I was encouraged to do that, and ultimately that led to a much greater freedom than just a political freedom. (Adams Interview, 2003)

One example of nonracialism involved Charles Humphries and Allie Fataar. Humphries had been in the South African army stationed in northern Africa in World War II, and because he was a teacher he was in charge of classes for soldiers. Part of the curriculum for these young white South African soldiers was what might be called nonracialism, as strange as it might sound for the South African government at the time. Two liberal professors, Ernest Malherbe and Leon Marquard, prepared a training pamphlet that used some of Marquard's book, *The Black Man's Burden*, as nonracial sensitivity training for the army. Humphries brought the pamphlet to the school along with the posters that accompanied it. Dudley recalled the moment including the fact that Allie Fataar used the posters as wallpaper in Room 13.

> My warning, my caveat, was that racism can flourish under any skin colour. Fascism can flourish under any skin colour, and we want democracy to flourish. Mr. Humphries had been in the war. He was classified as a white person, but he had a completely open attitude

> in regard to colour. He had been an education officer in the army and one of the tasks that he was given was to teach the soldiers what the educators in the army regarded as being reasonable, acceptable attitudes that would enable them to be accepted amongst so-called black people. They produced this manual to guide the education officers. In this guide they had a chapter on this whole question of blood and the idiocy of blood, blue blood, and so on, etc., pure blood, etc. . . . What is more, it was a challenging document because it said that there was no difference in the blood groupings that you found amongst the whites or found amongst the blacks, and that the blood taken from a black person could be given to a white person during the course of a blood transfusion provided the blood groupings were compatible. They had a line that I've mentioned to you, and I'll never forget that because I learned it from that manual, **"that racism is the last refuge of the small mind."** (Dudley Interview, 2003)

Politics was definitively part of Livingstone, and the roster of teachers that were members and officers of organizations on the left was formidable. The principal, Edward Roberts, was the chairperson of the Anti-CAD and president of the TLSA in the 1940s; Allie Fataar was the secretary of the TLSA and a respected orator in the NEF; Frank Grammer was a leading member of the Anti-CAD. That is not to mention Dudley and George Abrahams, who were becoming more and more important in each of the organizations including NEUM. Most of the black teachers on the faculty were members of the Claremont branch of the TLSA, and their politics was nurtured in their students, whom they invited to meetings and encouraged especially regarding nonracialism, but also with a sense of noncollaboration and even anti-imperialism. Albert Adams recalls going to Hosea Jaffe's house on Friday evenings for political discussions. This was before Jaffe taught at Livingstone. An example of acting on both noncollaboration and anti-imperialist beliefs came in 1947 when the English royal family visited Cape Town. The Education Department "asked" each school to bring their students to the honorary parade, and the teachers at Livingstone decided that the school should boycott the event. The boycott is a foreshadowing of things to come at Livingstone as well as the broader political resistance of both NEUM and the TLSA; it also might be the initial event that brought conflict to the school in the relationship between Roberts and his teacher/comrades.

Curriculum issues and the fact that he was involved in opposition politics brought problems with the Education Department for Edward Roberts. Dudley was involved first as his comrade and later as an adversary; the latter still saddens Dudley some today. Just before the apartheid regime came to power, Roberts was often called before the Education Department to defend policies at the school. He sometimes went to the department on his own or with colleagues to dispute departmental actions, and he was not appreciated for his work with African schools in Langa and the Cape African Teachers' Association. Dudley recalls joining Roberts at the Education Department in a dispute over anticipated changes in curriculum for coloured students. The meeting was just at the time when the Nationalist Party was coming to power.

> Mr. Roberts put the whole issue before them, and then Malan indicated to Mr. Roberts that he was wrong, that the department had no such intentions. Mr. Roberts listened very carefully and then said to him that we had learned this from your own inspectors. He also tackled this whole question of standards. Mr. Roberts landed into them and said to Malan that pupils must be taught on the basis of equality with everybody else in this country. I think that from that time onwards they realized that Mr. Roberts was not on their side. They wanted the principals of these schools to work along with them, and so when Mr. Roberts was deeply involved in this, they called him in and warned him. (Dudley Interview, 2003)

Dudley is convinced that in subsequent days as the apartheid regime took power, they summoned Edward Roberts and threatened him with dismissal and that would have meant losing his income and more importantly his pension, for which he had worked many years. A final event in Roberts's career portrays the noncollaborationist position of NEUM, the TLSA, and the faculty at Livingstone High School. Unfortunately, it also exemplifies the damage that apartheid imposed on black South Africans, in this case Edward Roberts.

Two years after the Nationalist Party came to power, the government began to plan a massive 1952 celebration of the 300th anniversary of Van Riebeeck coming to South Africa. Ironically, the 300th anniversary prompted Hosea Jaffe, who was a member of NEUM and often wrote in the organization's newspaper, *The Torch*, to write a history of colonialism and imperialism in South Africa titled *300 Years*. As we will discuss in Chapter Five, the TLSA, NEUM, the ANC, and other political organizations that opposed racism and apartheid protested loudly against the celebration. They called for boycotts within the context of the strong foundational principle of noncollaboration, and the faculty at Livingstone High School was part of the resistance. The government planned a massive celebration to honor Van Riebeeck and the Dutch occupation of the southern tip of Africa and the great legacy they left to their heirs, white South Africans. The Education Department expected all public schools to participate, with massive numbers of children turning out from white, coloured, Indian, and African schools to show the importance of the event to all South Africans.

The Education Department printed brochures that were to be distributed in the schools, and while the critical mass of Livingstone's faculty were clear in their opposition, it was a huge dilemma for Edward Roberts. Although he was a respected leader in opposition organizations, he feared the consequences in the Education Department, and he and a small number of teachers began to distribute the Van Riebeeck Day brochures. In addition, brochures were delivered to selected resistant teachers who Roberts must have thought might acquiesce. It was an incident with one of those teachers and Roberts that led to the final break between Roberts and the opposition faculty, his comrades in the political organizations. Roberts sent a student to the class of a math teacher, John Fife, to distribute brochures. Fife had attended Livingstone, and his family was actively involved in the school. He told the student to leave with the brochures. The incident is especially troublesome because Roberts reported Fife to the Education Department, and a hearing was held that concluded with Fife being transferred to a different school. A few teachers testified for Roberts, but most of the teachers stood behind John Fife. For the former it might have been loyalty as they had worked with Edward Roberts for many years and they trusted him both as an educator and opposition politico. The teachers who supported Fife agreed with his stand and were actively fighting against Van Riebeeck Day both in and out of school. It is interesting that Roberts would not have considered having brochures sent to the classrooms where Grammer, Fataar, or Dudley taught. As already noted, Richard Dudley is still saddened by the event. With many years of reflection he is clear on the dilemma that Roberts faced. At the time, however, he saw Roberts as turning against his own principles as well as those of NEUM and the TLSA—he was collaborating. Dudley vocally disagreed with Roberts at the school, and he and Fataar were also part of the Legal Aid Bureau of the TLSA that ruled Roberts had wronged Fife.

Roberts subsequently publicly reprimanded Dudley, and for the short time that Roberts remained at Livingstone before retiring, the school was rather tense and unpleasant. Part of the conflict was a mutual sense of betrayal, and the intensity of the situation was clear when Dudley and other teachers did not attend Roberts's retirement party. What they did do, however, was to lead students in boycotting and protesting against Van Riebeeck Day.

> We didn't attend any of the things that were arranged for the schools. I wrote certain of the propaganda pamphlets. I also approached people in different organizations about the fact that they should turn their backs upon this sort of thing. I said that as a teacher I cannot now in the light of my duties draw pupils into this sort of thing. We had parent-teacher associations so we had entrée amongst the parents. We got a great deal of support from them in that way. Well, within a matter of a fortnight we distributed something like

> about 500,000 pamphlets. We linked this opposition to this celebration to other issues. (Dudley Interview, 2003)

Dudley and his comrades wed education and politics. Studying science and English, or history and math, was connected to an understanding of oppression and racism—to nonracialism and noncollaboration. William Nasson analyzes it succinctly in his *Radical History* essay: "Above all, as socialists, they had an intuitive grasp of the primary value of history and of their own historical function. Whatever their specialist teaching subjects—history, literature, physics, or biology—they constituted a collective forum which molded a process of historically-aware learning among pupils" (Nasson, 1990, p. 190). Although Dudley's political education and participation were quite intense during his UCT years, his coming of age as a comrade corresponded with his early years as a teacher at Livingstone High School.

Becoming a Comrade

When Richard Dudley began his teaching career, he also became more involved in the New Era Fellowship. Besides organizing meetings and study groups, he recruited students and helped initiate fellowships in different areas of Cape Town as well as in places as far as Kimberley to the north and what is now called the Eastern Cape. While his responsibilities in NEF had quickly expanded, he grew even more appreciative of the lessons he learned from his elders.

> When you sat down with these people, you learned from them. You saw the breadth, because they were cultivated people, they weren't just activists. They had something to offer. What we were doing then was getting out of our cocoon and coming into a new world and looking at things differently. And it was on the basis of ideas, and not ideas that were sucked out of people's thumbs, because you could always relate this to the realities outside. We would take this sort of thing back into our study circles and then look at ourselves and say that the fact of the matter is that we are unique in this. We've got the opportunity of studying in this way and a hell of a lot of people don't. There were only 10 million people at that time in South Africa. Somehow or another we had to turn our way of looking at these things around. Because the generation before us who had these privileges reckoned that their degrees gave them status. You see this because in the publications that they put out they would always put their degrees behind their names. (Dudley Interview, 2003)

The latter part of the quote was a lesson quickly learned in NEF, and it carried over into both the TLSA and NEUM. Ideas and substance were important, labels and degrees were not. As part of a movement that was fighting for democracy for all people, it was imperative to have ideas, not pretense.

> They said that we shouldn't go and disport ourselves amongst people who had been denied an education by having these tags attached to our names. They said that we should rather by the quality of what we were able to put into society indicate to people that something had happened to us. We weren't going to tell them we've got degrees. We just had to show them the quality and the relevance of what we were doing and the extent to which we were prepared to sacrifice our time instead of going to pubs and dances and all the rest of it. So we undertook to follow this path and that was the nature of our blood oath. (Dudley Interview, 2003)

Dudley had become a student member of the Teachers' League of South Africa in his last year at the University, and he affiliated with the Anti-CAD and then the Non-European Unity Movement when the organization was launched in 1943. As has already been shown, membership in both NEF and NEUM included many TLSA teachers, and leadership positions in all three organizations overlapped. Dudley recalls that he often did not think about what group he was doing specific work for at a particular time because the issues always had to do with racism and oppression, and there was nonracial and noncollaborative work that needed to be done. The Anti-CAD and NEUM were both launched just before Dudley became a teacher, and the transformation of the TLSA was completed in the same time period. Dudley recalls Ben Kies coming to a NEF meeting and warning that the government was keen to set up a Coloured Affairs Department as a means to further segregate coloureds, just as they had previously done to Africans with legislation and the initiation of the Natives Representative Council. The reaction was that people in NEF introduced the Anti-CAD and quickly thereafter combined with the All African Convention to launch the Non-European Unity Movement.

In January 1943 the United Party government announced that they were going to act on the Wilcock Commission recommendations by forming the Cape Coloured Permanent Commission (CCPC) allegedly to "advise the Government on all matters affecting the economic, political and social interests of the Cape Coloured and Cape Malay communities" (Lewis, 1987, p. 209). By March the name of the commission was changed to the easier to refer to Coloured Advisory Council (CAC). Not surprisingly the reaction in the coloured community was swift. The African Peoples' Organization supported the CAC, and their president, Francis Gow, was named as the Chair of the Council. Serving with him were APO and TLSA stalwarts like George Golding and David van der Ross. Gow earnestly believed that the CAC would help the coloured community in terms of social welfare and education, and he stated conditions at the initial meeting in April 1943: "No segregation. No Coloured Affairs Department. No tampering with your votes. No introduction of measures affecting us without reference to the Council" (Lewis, 1987, p. 212). Gow and his colleagues on the Council must have not fully trusted Smuts and the United Party or the caveat would not have been necessary. On the other hand, they did believe that the Council would aid the lives of coloured South Africans with better health care, fuller employment, and improved housing and schools—a continuation of Rhodes's "civilized man."

The New Era Fellowship, of course, thought that CAC would help the government to do exactly what Gow's statement argued against. Goolam Gool and Ben Kies both said publicly that the government would follow the Natives Representative Council with a Coloured Affairs Department and Coloureds Representative Council, all with the aid of CAC. A month after the United Party announced CAC, members of the NEF, with the support of the Fourth International and the Communist Party of South Africa, launched the Anti-Coloured Affairs Department (Anti-CAD). The Anti-CAD immediately published pamphlets saying that CAC members were dupes because the purpose of the Council was the cooptation of black South Africans to facilitate further racial segregation and oppression. The Anti-CAD was extremely hard on CAC members, calling them traitors and quislings. They urged a boycott of CAC and published a note on dealing with the "quislings":

> Don't have any social or personal intercourse with them. Don't greet them. Don't have any conversation with them. Don't visit them, and don't invite them to your home. Don't meet them, even if it is necessary to cross over to the other side of the street. Don't see them, even if you do come face to face with them. (Lewis, 1987, p. 214)

In April 1943 more than 2,000 people gathered in Cape Town to protest CAC and vowed to fight against the Council as well as the predicted coming of a Coloured Affairs Department. There was a second meeting the following month where Ben Kies illustrated the goals of both the state and the nonracial, noncollaboration resistance. Kies argued that the marriage of British imperialism and South African capitalism lived on the backs of black South Africans, and that institutions like the Natives Representatives Council and the coming Coloured Affairs Department were means of divide and rule. He proposed a coalition of non-Europeans to fight against capitalism and imperialism, class disparity and racism. "We must take the road of unity. We must unite the struggles of oppressed Africans, oppressed Coloured, oppressed Indian, into the unified struggle of the oppressed Non-European.

We must build up a real and militant United Front of the PEOPLE." (Kies, p. 12)

The Anti-CAD tried to organize a boycott of the 1944 election. Although many people were distrustful of the Coloured Advisory Council, they feared the election of Nationalist Party candidates more, so the boycott was a failure and extremely disappointing for those resisting on the left. CAC helped initiate some changes in education and employment opportunities and viewed their work as important, but with successes came more sellouts in terms of distinguishing between coloureds and Africans. The people on CAC supported influx control and viewed themselves as victorious when they were able to limit employment access for Africans—exactly the divide and rule of blacks that the New Era Fellowship, Anti-CAD, and other organizations abhorred.

Because of the Coloured Advisory Council, the voices of nonracial, noncollaborationist politics in South Africa grew louder. The Anti-CAD organization joined with the All African Convention (AAC) in 1943 to form the Non-European Unity Movement (NEUM). It was also at this time that the Teachers' League of South Africa transformed into an organization that wed education and politics with the same nonracial, noncollaboration ideology of NEUM. Dudley became deeply involved in both organizations as a member and officer, and much of his teaching and political life therafter occurred within the context of his life in both NEUM and the TLSA. Ideologically NEUM represented the positions presented by Ben Kies in his "The Background of Segregation" talk at the May 1943 Anti-CAD meeting. Launched in Bloemfontein in December 1943, the Non-European Unity Movement immediately stated a theoretical foundation, as presented in our introduction, of a nonnegotiable belief in nonracialism and noncollaboration. Both political and academic critiques of NEUM have argued that the organization's nonnegotiable policies, sometimes viewed as stubbornness, kept NEUM from having a larger influence, some would say any influence, on South African resistance politics. At the first meeting, in keeping with nonracialism and the federated nature of the organization, Tengo Jabavu and Goolam Gool were elected president and vice president. Isaac Tabata and Ben Kies wielded great influence, however, in the organization. NEUM drafted a Ten Point Programme of minimum demands that included the vote, free compulsory education for all children, and other freedoms with no distinctions of race, color, or gender. (Lewis, 1987, pp. 221, 222)

The values and beliefs of the Non-European Unity Movement, including a nonracial system and equality of all people, are evident in the Ten Point Programme. NEUM had some early successes, but the organization was not able to make alliances with other organizations like the ANC, CPSA, or the South African Indian Congress (SAIC). NEUM was able to influence changes in the APO where Gow was defeated for the presidency, and the organization began to support NEUM initiatives. Because so many members were teachers, NEUM also helped to facilitate progressive changes in the TLSA.

In the mid- to late-1930s, although the Teachers' League of South Africa was still very much a moderate body, there began to be some tension surrounding its policy of being nonpolitical as well as the insistence that it was a coloured organization. As we discussed earlier, the APO struggled with its position on racialism in the 1920s and early 1930s, but the TLSA did not appear to have the same challenges. The Teachers' League had rejected approaches from African teachers, but for some reason in 1934 it accepted applications from a small number of Africans and changed the constitution so that it no longer limited membership to coloured teachers (Adhikari, 2005, p. 95). At the end of the decade the TLSA also changed its policy of accepting the Education Department edict for different curriculums for specific ethnic groups. The change might have been precipitated by a textbook that was written by two members of the organization, Dorothy Hendricks, who taught at Zonnebloem Training College, and Christian Viljoen, who taught at Athlone Institute in Paarl. The text was titled *The Student Teacher's History Course: For the Use in Coloured Training Colleges*. Adhikari explains that the book follows the colonial and racist tradition of presenting images of happy slaves and shows a denigrated view of coloured people that he argues it would have to do for Education Department approval (Adhikari, 2005, pp. 39–41).

A final example of the APO-like contradictions in the late-1930s Teachers' League is seen in the pages of the *Educational Journal*. In his 1937 Presidential Address Edward Roberts spoke of solutions for coloured poverty and lack of progress, but a colleague, Ernest Moses, forcibly presented the culture of poverty position of the TLSA in the journal, listing coloured traits as "immorality, drunkenness, hooliganism, gambling, and extravagance" (Adhikari, 2005, pp. 84, 85). Although Roberts had spoken of coloured backwardness in 1937, he was compelled to lash out at Moses: "It is astonishing to find men, good and sensible . . . who consider hybrid people as possessed of vices only, with no virtues . . . [and] relegate the hybrid people to the lowly position of hewers of wood and drawers of water" (Adhikari, 2005, p. 85). So even before the overt conflict between moderates and NEF, Anti-CAD, and NEUM teachers engulfed the TLSA, there were intimations of progressive change in the organization. Willem van Schoor, who later became president of TLSA and in 1951 wrote one of its classic political tracts, "The Origin and Development of Segregation in South Africa," led a challenge at the 1938 conference of a motion supporting stricter segregation between coloureds and Africans. He also asked the organization to formally challenge Education Department policies. Admitting African members, resisting differential curriculum, challenging culture of poverty racism, and confronting the moderate old guard was not the 1920s Teachers' League of South Africa.

By 1943 Anti-CAD members were active in many local branches of the TLSA, and left-leaning teachers from Livingstone dominated the Claremont branch. Kies, van Schoor, and Fataar were all members of the Executive. The Anti-CAD takeover began in earnest, however, at the 1943 conference in Kimberly. There had been continuing conflict, with both the moderates and radicals attacking each other through articles in the *Educational Journal*. The radicals disrupted the conference by publicly confronting members of the Executive who had taken a positive position on CAC. The moderates won the elections, although Lewis alludes to some inconsistencies in the voting process. It was the winners, however, who left the organization in 1944 to form their own teachers' association, the Teachers' Educational and Professional Association, with the purpose of working with the United Party government and the Education Department. The "young turks," as Allie Fataar called himself and his comrades, had won the Teachers' League of South Africa.

Dudley's older sisters were members of the TLSA, and they brought him to the Claremont branch as an associate, or student, member in 1943. His future wife, Iris Atkins, was already in the TLSA, as she had completed her training at Saint Augustine Teacher Training College in 1941 and was teaching primary school in Salt River. Dudley made his first contribution to the TLSA in 1943 during the struggle for the Teachers' League between moderates and progressives.

> I remember actually doing a job for them. The battle inside the League at that time was a pretty furious one, and there was a chap Arthur Petersen who was the President of the Teachers' League. When he delivered the presidential address I happened to get a copy of it, and I remembered reading this address in the university before he delivered it. I found out that it was actually the address that had been given by the President of the South African Teachers Association—a nun who was then president. It was in the *Journal in Education*. So I went that afternoon, I cycled down to Claremont and there were some of the chaps who were busy with organizational matters for the League, and I gave them religion. That was my first major contribution. (Dudley Interview, 2003)

Although Dudley had already begun to participate in New Era Fellowship intellectual and political discussions and debates at Stakesby-Lewis Hostel in District Six, much of his initial work consisted of pamphleteering and papering walls with anti-CAC posters, along with Iris Atkins and other young members. This work was done in Cape Town but also in rural communities outside of Cape Town such as Grabow, Stellenbosch, and Paarl. The interaction between the TLSA, Anti-CAD, NEF, and NEUM is apparent as they were all committed to the same cause. In the Teachers' League specifically, Dudley and his comrades helped prepare and distribute copies of the *Educational Journal*. Dudley's apprenticeship, shall we say, was short-lived. He is fond of saying that he never had a childhood because he entered the University of Cape Town at a very young age, was politicized early, was given too much responsibility very quickly at Livingstone, and finally was vaulted into leadership positions in both the Teachers' League of South Africa and the Non-European Unity Movement just a couple of years after joining each organization. In 1945 he was elected to the Executive of the TLSA and was also appointed to the editorial board of the *Educational Journal*. Fortunately, he had mentoring from Livingstone colleagues like Fataar, Grammer, and Roberts. He reflected on what he learned at the University and in the New Era Fellowship to help him take on tasks at a young age.

> It helps you to understand that you don't know enough. You don't want to be embarrassed, so you read like hell and you attend all the instructional meetings that are held. I was promoted into inner circles, and I must say I took very serious notice of what was being taught there—those inner circle meeting discussions of the events in South Africa. The people who were introducing these discussions had themselves, of course, a better background then myself. They also had the methodology, so you could learn a hell of a lot from them. (Dudley Interview, 2003)

As an editor of the *Educational Journal*, Dudley was expected to produce articles on political and educational issues of the time. Since there were not boundaries between the organizations, he also became involved in management and writing for the Non-European Unity Movement's paper, *The Torch*. Launched in 1946, the newspaper was published until 1964, when apartheid suppression accelerated in South Africa. *The Torch* was an eight-page publication named after the Bolshevik publication *Iskra* and it was initially distributed throughout the country (Adhikari, 2005, p. 104). The inaugural issue stated the paper's purpose, and unsurprisingly it mirrored the mission of NEUM. The paper promised to support the fight for full democratic rights for all South Africans. Dudley wrote on science and sport and covered court cases against black South Africans. Initially five people—Allie Fataar, Randolph Fowler, Salie Edross, Ben Kies, and Dudley—worked together writing, managing, publishing, and distributing *The Torch*. Joan Kay and Joyce Meissenheimer, the head girl prefect and schoolmate of Dudley at Livingstone, co-edited the newspaper until they were banned, and other people helped on particular projects. For example, Iris Dudley became involved in the publication and spent a great deal of time reading and editing galleys.

Dudley stressed that the publishing of both the *Educational Journal* and *The Torch* were group efforts; it was a team that fought for equality and democracy producing publications as well as doing much of the other emancipation work. Both the journal and newspaper sometimes carried bylines, but *The Torch* and the *Educational Journal* were collective efforts. When apartheid grew harsher in the mid-1950s and 1960s, anonymity was also important because extreme consequences sometimes met verbal resistance. Dudley explained the process as he reflected on some of the important political pamphlets.

> We had a pamphlet on *Black Consciousness*, that little pamphlet? Not under my hand? Yes, and then the other one—*Majority Rule*—that was also a collective effort, but there was one person who was acting as scribe, and there were others who added particular portions when it was felt that they could do it effectively without destroying the continuity and the fluidity. (Dudley Interview, 2003)

As editor of the *Educational Journal* and because of his analytical expertise, Ben Kies would often write editorials in both the journal and the newspaper. But as Dudley makes clear, they were dissected and critiqued and edited by other comrades.

While Dudley took the duties of editorial writing over from Kies in the late 1940s when the latter won a British Council Scholarship and went to study in London, the common thinking was to present the voice of the collective, quite consistent, one would think, with the socialism that was espoused. While there were certainly people in both the TLSA and NEUM who were self-centered and wanted personal glory, Dudley and other Teachers' Leaguers worked as comrades. Being a team joins nonracialism and noncollaboration as tenets of both the TLSA and NEUM, and examples are apparent throughout their twentieth-century work. In fact, in the final chapter we will see that the theme is very much alive in Dudley's life at the present time.

Although the Non-European Unity Movement is criticized as quickly becoming a coloured organization, up until the time members were banned in the 1960s there were branches throughout the country, and there was the continuing alliance of the Anti-CAD and the All African Convention. In education the alliance was between the TLSA and the Cape African Teachers' Association. Again, there are questions to be asked about the depth of this alliance, but Dudley views it as part of his nonracial and noncollaborative work starting in the 1940s and continuing with even greater urgency during the apartheid years. Alongside of Isaac Tabata, he worked with teachers in the rural Ciskei and Transkei, now the Eastern Cape, and made strong connections locally with colleagues and comrades who taught at Langa High School. In addition, in the 1950s joint programs were launched between Livingstone and Langa High School. As 1948 and the coming of the apartheid era approached, both NEUM and the TLSA expanded their work. Dudley and his comrades tried to extend the mission of both organizations beyond the boundaries of Cape Town through the publications and meetings and visits. But there were ominous signs, both in the public statements on segregation by Malan and the Nationalist Party and in the growing disparity and racial segregation in the country. Specifically in Cape Town, educational and occupational disparities had grown as greater numbers of whites graduated from high school while both skilled labor and professional positions for blacks had abated (Bickford-Smith, van Heyningen, Worden, 1999, pp. 121, 122). In addition, more and more public places were beginning to enforce segregation. While this would intensify greatly in the early 1950s, the late 1940s saw segregated parks, beaches, swimming pools, and public toilets (Bickford-Smith, van Heyningen, Worden, 1999, p. 125). Finally, although there were still integrated neighborhoods, the government had begun to build segregated housing after World War II, and of course class continued to create segregation. Although Dudley and his comrades initially viewed the coming of apartheid as just an expansion of the ongoing twentieth-century oppression and racism in South Africa, they would quickly understand that the expansion was actually an intense magnification. Dudley's and his comrades' fight for democracy in the early years of apartheid through Sharpeville—in both society and education—is portrayed in the next chapter.

FIGURE 1. Richard Dudley *(George Hallet photographer)*

FIGURE 2. Russell, Nerine, Gary Dudley—Nerine's graduation (*Photo courtesy of the Dudley family*)

FIGURE 3. Alleta Dudley (*Photo courtesy of the Dudley family*)

FIGURE 4. Iris, Nerine, Richard Dudley—Nerine's graduation (*Photo courtesy of the Dudley family*)

FIGURE 5. Nerine, Richard, Iris Dudley *(Photo courtesy of the Dudley family)*

FIGURE 6. Dudley family portrait *(Photo courtesy of the Dudley family)*

FIGURE 7. Samuel Dudley (*Photo courtesy of the Dudley family*)

FIGURE 8. Richard Dudley—Groundbreaking (*Photo courtesy of the Dudley family*)

FIGURE 9. Allie Fataar *(Photo courtesy of Aslam Fataar)*

FIGURE 10. Tom Hanmer *(Photo courtesy of the Hanmer family)*

FIGURES 11 and 12. *(above)* Livingstone High School staff photo (1959), *(below)* staff photo 1969

FIGURE 13. Livingstone High School staff photo 1979
First Row: Bolivar, Mchachlan, Carlier, Esterheizen, Evans, Dudley, Rash, Lewis. Second Row: Banda, Springveldt, Dewes, Lehy, McArthur, Bardien, Coults, Hicks, Middlemost, Kida, du Plooy, Peterson. Third Row: Kannemeyer, Esau, Fauodien, Newman, Zyl, Darmalingam, Hendricks, Petersen, Newman, Spangeberg, Grifiths, Kingwell, Currie

FIGURE 14. Staff photo 1989

5

education for democracy I

The Early Years of Apartheid through Sharpeville

On more than one occasion, Richard Dudley mentioned that apartheid came as no surprise because it was a continuation of the oppression and segregation that had dominated South Africa throughout the twentieth century. In addition, the Nationalist Party and its leader, D. F. Malan, had been upping the ante of racist rhetoric throughout the 1940s. Immediately after the election, the *Educational Journal* published an article, "Apartheid in Education," penned by Allie Fataar, making a similar argument. The Non-European Unity Movement publicly asserted that the apartheid regime would simply be a new version of the imperialist-capitalist model. They were wrong. But it might be that no one could have imagined that the Nationalist Party would win eleven straight national elections between 1948 and 1992, or that the apartheid government would so vehemently and viciously pass and enforce laws that strengthened and magnified the segregation of white, Indian, African, and coloured people in South African society, with whites, of course, on top.

Malan did not hide the party's intentions as the plan was presented to the South African public during the 1948 election campaign. Besides explaining that the Natives Representative Council would be extended and that segregation of Africans—now to be called Bantus—would be exacerbated with enforcement of reserves or homelands as well as punitive measures for Africans in urban areas, the Nationalist Party also campaigned on further separation of Indians and coloureds. For coloured South Africans who lived primarily in Cape Town and the Western Cape, that meant banning sexual contact and marriage between coloureds and whites, public segregation, separate education, segregated housing, loss of voting rights, and the coming of a Coloureds Representative Council. The promises made by the Nationalist Party were all fulfilled by the mid-1960s. In the early apartheid years legislation included the Population Registration Act (1950), Group Areas Act (1950), Immorality Act (1950), Suppression of Communism Act (1950), and Bantu Authorities Act (1951), that not only classified people as African, coloured, Indian, or white but also designated where one was allowed to live, work, or attend school because of the color of one's skin. In many places African, coloured, and Indian people were literally taken out of their family homes and forced to relocate to designated areas, often far from city centers and workplaces. Education laws like the Bantu Education Act (1953), the Coloured Persons Education Act (1963), and the Indian Education Act (1965) assured that children attended school only with people of their own color. The apartheid regime was committed to a totally segregated society—politically, socially, economically, and educationally, as well as culturally. So in spite of socialist analysis from NEUM and government racist ideology and legislation prior to 1948, the legislation and actions of the apartheid regime would change the life of Richard Dudley and his comrades in the Non-European Unity Movement and Teachers' League of South Africa, forever.

Dudley's home, school, and public life became very different in the 1950s. While apartheid had an overwhelming effect, it is also important to report that he got married and started a family while at the same time expanding his role and responsibility at Livingstone High School and the TLSA. Iris Atkins and Richard Dudley married in May 1948 after he received permission from her parents. Her father commented that he wondered when they would marry, because they had known each other for eleven years and had been together for at least seven. Iris Dudley laughed as she recalled that he did not have any money, only books. After their marriage they moved into her parents' home, and her parents moved to the house of one of her sisters. They raised their children on York Street, just blocks from Livingstone High School, until they were forced to move in 1972 under the Group Areas Act.

Iris Dudley taught for less than two years just after her marriage and then had their first child, Nerine, in 1950. There were problems when Nerine was young because she was afflicted with very bad asthma and had to be taken for extended periods to drier climates because the Cape Town humidity caused her great suffering. Initially that meant an extended stay in Kimberley with her mother while her father remained at his teaching post in Cape Town. The complexities of the time included Dudley's political involvement, but also his extended responsibilities as the acting principal of Livingstone High School beginning in 1953. That particular appointment was connected to apartheid, as was his rejection when he considered taking a teaching post in Kimberley to be with Iris and Nerine.

> At that time something else cropped up in my life because our daughter, who was about three or four years of age, was terribly affected by asthma, and we became quite desperate. I had wanted, actually, to leave to go up to Kimberley for a dry climate. I had applied for a post there and was selected for the job, strangely enough, by a school board that consisted mainly of people who had come from the United Party. Kimberley was a United Party stronghold, and despite the fact that they had people on the board who knew of my activities in the Anti-CAD Movement and the Unity Movement, they actually voted in favor to my appointment. But when it came down to Malan at the department, he turned it down. (Dudley Interview, 2003)

In retrospect it is very difficult to imagine Richard Dudley living his life anywhere but Cape Town, and the idea of him living in Kimberley is incomprehensible. Needless to say, there is power in family and children. Nerine's health improved somewhat as she got older, and Dudley's life at Livingstone changed dramatically. While he is fond of saying that Edward Roberts pushed him too quickly and beyond his maturity in the late 1940s, it is when Roberts retired after the Van Riebeeck Day fiasco that Dudley's responsibilities at the school really changed. He had worked with Fataar and Grammer under Roberts on scheduling and other management tasks, but in 1953 he was named acting principal at the school before his thirtieth birthday. The irony is that in subsequent years when he was actually the best person for the job, the department would not consider him for the position.

Fataar, Grammer, and Ray Carlier were all more senior and qualified than Dudley at the time but were passed over for the position. Dudley believes that Grammer was the logical choice, but both he and Fataar were more senior in opposition politics than Dudley, and that might have been an issue for the Education Department. In addition, Grammer was vocal in his criticism of Roberts during the Van Riebeeck controversy. In the case of Ray Carlier, even though she would become the principal later in the decade, at the time there were no women high school principals, so gender might have been an issue. Interestingly, when Iris Dudley spoke about meetings of the TLSA, she said that women made cakes and served tea at the meetings, and although she is not at all accusatory, her recollections do make one stop and question the place of gender at the time, not only at the Education Department, but also in left-wing political groups. While Helen Kies has been a prominent member of the Teachers' League for many years as well as the longtime editor of the *Educational Journal*, we might ask whether, within the movement at the time, was she viewed more as the wife of Ben Kies than as a politico in her own right. There is a 2004 South African book called *Men Behaving Differently* that argues that there have been great changes in issues of gender discrimination since 1994. Some of the younger activists might disagree. Vivienne Carelse, a leader in the progressive South African Democratic Teachers' Union (SADTU) in the 1980s and currently the Director of Education and Public Programmes at Iziko Museums of Cape Town, commented that "the Education Department used to be led by pale males, but today it is led by not-so-pale males." (Carelse Interview, 1999)

When the 1953 school year began, Livingstone High School did not have a principal, and the School Committee, made up of six parents including two strong and vocal women, got the approval of the department to appoint Dudley on an interim basis. He would serve from April 1953 until the end of 1955. Dudley described the tone of the school from the end of World War II into the 1950s:

> I would say that, for want of a better term, the general atmosphere that prevailed at the school was oppositional. But it wasn't just that. I think that an independence in the ideas, in the philosophy within which framework people conducted their work at school, was pretty well established. This school would act as a bastion against the kinds of things that the United Party had hoped to install in 1945 when they introduced the Coloured Education Ordinance. (Dudley Interview, 1999)

There were changes on the staff at the time that continued through the 1950s. Dudley believes that the faculty became stronger both academically and politically during the decade. Livingstone was known as a Teachers' League school, and one of the people who joined the teaching staff in the period when Dudley was acting principal was his political comrade Hosea Jaffe, who had just finished his book *300 Years*. Unlike Dudley and his other TLSA comrades at the school, Jaffe did not have any administrative duties, so he was able to spend a great deal of time meeting with students, and he taught them and nurtured them politically. Livingstone became more political as apartheid showed its face, passing further racist legislation and putting more pressure on schools to facilitate the apartheid regime. The school's boycott of the Van Riebeeck Festival, introduced in the previous chapter, provides portraits of Dudley's and Livingstone's opposition education and politics as well as the broad nonracial resistance of the left towards the festival.

Cultural Apartheid

Earlier in the chapter, culture was included in a listing of the many elements of segregation legislated and enforced by the apartheid regime. It was very important for the Nationalist Party to infuse in all white Afrikaners, especially poor Afrikaners, that white was high and black was low, no matter where you stood in the class strata. In the name of Afrikaner Christian Nationalism, the Nationalist Party continually propagandized poor Afrikaners, inculcating the belief that they were victims of British capitalism as well as uncivilized blacks, in spite of the fact that they were racially superior.

> In the 1940s, as growing African urbanization fuelled fears of oorstroming, it became expedient for Afrikaner ideologues to emphasize the ethnic 'purity' of Afrikaners and the imperative of protecting this purity against miscegenation with ostensibly inferior indigenous races. Consequently, as the reverse side of the coin of aggressive Afrikaner nationalism, NP ideologues formulated an explicit and insulting version of racism, which crystallized into the policy of apartheid. The NP regarded the different African ethnic groups as heathen nations to be Christianised and civilized by Afrikaners. White English-speakers were portrayed as people with dubious moral standards, permeated by the materialistic and egotistic values of capitalism. (Terreblanche, 2002, pp. 298, 299)

While this is not the moment to comment on the economic contradictions of this portrayal and apartheid to come, it suggests reasons why the Nationalist government was keen to celebrate the 300th anniversary of apartheid's hero in 1952. The purpose of the festival was to exemplify and solidify white superiority and separateness of the races, past and present. Leslie Witz expands on the theme in his extensive writing on the festival and black resistance.

> The primary purpose of the 1952 Jan van Riebeeck Festival revolved around establishing a sense of European-derived settler unity in South Africa, and thereby constructing a white racial 'national' identity. There was a pageant of past in the streets of Cape Town where floats symbolized the coming together of the 'civilized' settler nation breaking free of the shackles of 'Darkest Africa.' A massive festival fair was erected on Cape Town's foreshore, with the contrasts between 'native' primitiveness and European derived progress as its central motif. The convergence of Europeaness in South Africa and the divergence from 'nativeness' were carried forward in a range of other festival productions: the dances and performances in the festival stadium, the plays in the theatres, the displays in museums, the documentary newsreels, the imaginative descriptions by radio commentators and the numerous books and pamphlets that were published. Through all these productions the organizers of the festival envisaged that they were setting in place a "bastion of the White races at earth's extremist end." (Witz, 1998, pp. 187, 188)

As we discussed in the previous chapter, the Education Department expected black schools to participate in the festival. In fact, at Langa High School the story was similar to Livingstone, as the teachers who belonged to the Cape African Teachers' Association, a sister organization of the Teachers' League of South Africa, reacted with disdain when their principal suggested that the school participate. Dudley worked with his colleagues to organize a boycott of the event, and teachers at the school used the event to analyze false representations of history. Along with TLSA comrades, he wrote pamphlets promoting a boycott and visited schools and organization meetings to argue against participating in the Van Riebeeck Festival. The boycott went beyond noncollaboration because it also provided a very tangible teaching moment on racism, past and present. Livingstone was joined by many other black schools in boycotting the event. For example, fifteen predominantly coloured schools in Athlone and schools in the African township of Langa refused to participate. Besides black schools, students at UCT and many political organizations worked hard in opposition to the Van Riebeeck Festival. The Unity Movement made a public statement in *The Torch*:

> The main reasons for boycotting this orgy of Herrenvolkism are that the national oppression and exploitation of the Non-Whites are to be celebrated, that the triumph of the Master-Race over Kaffir, Hotnot and Coolies is to be celebrated, that another 300 years of domination are to be heralded. No matter what form these celebrations take, no matter how wonderful the exhibits and processions and sideshows, nothing can disguise the fact that the Herrenvolk is dancing and reveling upon our own enslavement. And only the slaves among us could consciously and voluntarily join them. (Witz, 2003, pp. 152, 153)

Political Resistance

Opposition teaching, pamphleteering, and meetings culminated in a counterdemonstration on the Parade just across the street from Van Riebeeck Festival activities. Although there was conflict between the ANC and NEUM at the time, the organizations appeared to drop their disputes to protest the event. Speakers like Cissie Gool and Johnny Gomas, who were now part of the Franchise Action Council (FRAC), an ANC affiliate, joined NEUM regulars Hosea Jaffe and Ben Kies on the podium to denounce the event as well as the apartheid regime. The latter group spoke of world politics and the divide-and-rule policy of the South African government, but they could not help but mention that the Non-European Unity Movement was the real builder of a nonracial nation. With humor Cissie Gool spoke of the one float that was missing, the Float of Truth, and Gomas spoke boldly of the ANC Defiance Campaign.

The *Cape Times* reported that blacks did not attend the festival. Although nonattendance was not exclusively due to the boycott, there is no question that teachers and activists were successful in their opposition. NEUM vowed to extend the boycott to the segregated spectator stands at the rugby stadium in Newlands. Throughout the 1950s and 1960s segregation became more prominent, and enforcement was harsh. Through the TLSA, however, many coloured South Africans in Cape Town lived with boycott as part of their everyday ethos. For example, some movie theaters allowed black people to sit only in the balcony, while other institutions might have one showing or certain times for blacks. The whole concept of racially being less of a person, however, was never accepted by NEUM or the TLSA, and examples of personal boycott are ever present. Jean September told me a story from her elementary school teaching days in the early 1980s that provides a powerful example. September's parents were members of the nonracial South African Committee on Sport (SACOS), and she came of age during the struggle and was affiliated with SADTU and the United Democratic Front (UDF). She and a colleague started a drama program at their school, and students, families, teachers, and the community attended productions.

> In the four years we put on three plays at school which were quite big productions. Because it was the first school in Mitchells Plain to put on a dramatic production, we were asked to have it staged at the Nico Malan. Now the Nico Malan is the theatre where only on certain days were "people of colour" allowed to go. For the rest of the time, only whites were allowed to go to the theatre. And it was also one of those symbols of apartheid that I've never ever gone to. It was a principled decision not to go to places where people were excluded. We were faced at school with putting on this production at the Nico Malan, and we refused. So it was the whole thing of being insubordinate, and we were going to be taken to the department, and we were going to have little black marks made against our names. It was a principled position and in the end we knew they wouldn't be able to pull it off, so they declined the offer. (September Interview, 1999)

For the ANC, the boycott of the Van Riebeeck Festival was part of launching the organization as the most important opposition group in South Africa. In 1950 the ANC, along with the South African Indian Congress (SAIC) and FRAC, began to plan a mass campaign against the laws of apartheid. The government was sent demands to repeal racist laws by February 1952 with an ultimatum that refusal would mean massive demonstrations, boycotts, and work actions by the ANC and other opposition organizations. Malan did not consider the demands, but he did take the time to scold the ANC for not going through appropriate channels—the Natives Representative Council. Arrogance and power were clearly evident, but the government's dismissal made people like Mandela and Sissulu and Oliver Tambo even more resolved. The Van Riebeeck Festival was used as a vehicle to announce the Defiance Campaign as April 6 was recognized as a National Day of Pledge and Prayer. There were meetings to launch the campaign in Cape Town as well as other cites and towns throughout the country, and June 26 was announced as the formal starting date of the Defiance Campaign. For several years actions were taken with exceptional success in the Eastern Cape, an area with a long ANC history and the birthplace of Nelson Mandela. Membership in the organization grew to well over 100,000 and the campaigns led to the formation of the opposition Congress and the writing of the now-famous Freedom Charter in 1955. In his book on the African National Congress Saul Dubow argues that this was the time that the ANC convincingly became the voice of opposition in South Africa, because it was the first black organization, with maybe the exception of the short-lived Industrial and Commercial Workers Union, that organized and executed a national political action campaign.

There are questions to be asked about why NEUM and the ANC never joined as opposition organizations and why NEUM did not become part of Congress. The acrimony had been quite bad when there were talks in 1948 between the AAC and the ANC, and Tabata personally had an intense conflict with members of the ANC when he was politicizing in Langa in the same year. Accusations have been made from both sides, and members of NEUM suggest that the ANC was too willing to collaborate, having ties to people like Sam Kahn from the CPSA, who served on the Natives Representative Council, and devoting too much time to actions that were more show than substance. As Lewis has noted, NEUM often called the actions of other left opposition groups "adventurism" (Lewis, 1987, p. 266). Accusations as explanation, of course, is too easy. Dudley himself made trips to Johannesburg to try and persuade comrades in the ANC to commit to the minimum demands of the Ten Point Programme, but it was Tabata who tried hard to negotiate a common ground, including his now well-known letter to Mandela. Ciraj Rassool discusses the letter that for Tabata became an anthem that at least partially defined the Unity Movement as "a turning point in the organisational history of the African people" (Rassool, 2004, p. 364). Tabata tried to persuade Mandela that the ANC Youth League was different than their elders as he accused the ANC of promoting a "theory of inferiority and trusteeship, with all its political manifestations" (Rassool, 2004, p. 364).

While Dudley believes that the ANC must have viewed him and his comrades as "obdurate and obstinate," Nasson explains that they were clearly unbending, and the official publications of the NEUM at the time did accuse the ANC of being reformist and questioned its official representation of African people. One is left to think that it would have never been a case of NEUM joining the Congress, but rather Congress joining NEUM, need more be said.

Bantu Education

Dudley worked hard on the boycott and committed both his teaching and political work to fighting the apartheid regime. He and his TLSA comrades were shaken when vocal African teachers were removed from their jobs in the early years of apartheid. Three young radical teachers from Orlando High School in the Johannesburg township of Soweto, Zeph Mothopeng, Eskia Mphahlele, and Isaac Matlhare, were elected as officers of the Transvaal African Teachers Association in 1951. They challenged the government's Eiselen Report and the coming of unequal Bantu Education (Hyslop, 1999, pp. 34–38; Mphahlele, 1978, pp. 156, 157). Shortly after the Nationalist Party came to power, they initiated what was to become the Eiselen Commission to study black education in South Africa. People of color were educated primarily in mission schools before apartheid, and the schools were under-resourced; there was much to be criticized in terms of facilities, teaching, standards, and general academics. After the report was released, the Bantu Education Act (1953) was passed initiating separate education for African children. Dudley and his comrades were quite clear that separate education acts for all blacks—coloureds and Indians—would follow, and the government formed a Commission on Coloured Education (1953) that led to the Coloured Persons Education Act (1963) and the Indian Education Act (1965).

Two essays in Kallaway's 1984 collection, *Apartheid and Education*, one by Frank Molteno and a second by Pam Christie and Colin Collins, connect Bantu Education with the coming of the African homelands, Bantustans. Christie and Collins cite Verwoerd's infamous 1954 speech:

> There is no place for him in the European community above the level of certain forms of labour. Within his own community, however, all doors are open. For that reason it is of no avail for him to receive a training which has as its aim absorption in the European community, where he cannot be absorbed. Until now he has been subjected to a school system which drew him away from his own community and misled him by showing him the green pastures of European society in which he was not allowed to graze. (Kallaway, 1984, p. 173)

There was resistance to Bantu Education, and the three teachers introduced above, Mothopeng, Mphahlele, and Matlhare, were very much involved. In their capacity as TATA officers they visited other African schools and held two conferences condemning the Eiselen Report. Zeph Mothopeng was a fiery orator, and Eskia Mphahlele had written against separate curriculums in the *Down Second Avenue*. Jonathan Hyslop reports in *The Classroom Struggle* that the principal of Orlando High School, Godfrey Nakane, was a supporter of Bantu Education and that he did not take kindly to teacher opposition. Nakane reported Mothopeng, Mphahlele, and Matlhare to the Education Department, and they were sacked from their jobs as teachers. Again, Mphahlale tells the story in his book *Down Second Avenue*. On more than one occasion Dudley has told me that Mphahlale had reported that Mandela, his neighbor in the early 1950s, said that education was not of immediate relevance to the struggle. Needless to say, Mphahlale disagreed as did Dudley and his comrades. They wrote endless *Educational Journal* articles against Bantu Education, with Dudley himself having bylines in 1952 and twice in 1953. In 1955 the *Journal* was no longer printing bylines for fear of government reprisals, but it did publish a pamphlet using real names in which Dudley was a participant. Dudley's 1952 article, "Ideals in Education," (May/June 1952, pp. 5, 6) critiqued the racist commonplaces used by the Eiselen Commission and chastised his former teacher at the University, Edward Pells, among others. As in much of Dudley's writing, he used literature as well as social, political, and economic sources. For this article it was Oscar Wilde's *Dorian Grey*. His 1953 article argued that Bantu Education was the antithesis of education, and he savaged the minister as an oppressive dictator (September 1953, pp. 5, 6). Dudley urged parents not to participate in the sham of Bantu Education or any Bantustan institutions and argued that the government use of education to separate people and create cheap labor was essentially evil. "The essential props of the Eiselen or de Vos Malan school will be the regimentation of the lives of the parents in a manner reminiscent of the pattern of Nazi and fascist education before WWII" (Dudley, September 1953, p. 34).

While the bannings were sobering and surely a foreshadowing of things to come in coloured education, many African teachers continued to teach content and resistance in the schools in spite of the great inequalities of Bantu education and personal repression. These African teachers represented a model for people in the TLSA as the government prepared to pass the Coloured Persons Education Act (1963).

Education and Politics

At Livingstone High School the faculty worked at blending teaching and politics during Dudley's tenure as acting principal. Throughout the apartheid years they reminded the students that the government believed that they were inferior, even though they of course were not. In addition, the teachers constantly explained to students how privileged they were to be getting a high school education and how important it would be for them to use their education to better society—to help create an egalitarian South Africa that at the very least practiced the Ten Point Programme. The message goes back to Ben Kies speaking to Dudley and other young members of the New Era Fellowship in the middle of the 1940s on how fortunate they were and how great their responsibility was to better society. Dudley was graphic when he spoke to his students on how the government wanted to link coloured education and work:

> The government in this country wants the boys in the class here to go and work on the farms. My job is to keep them off the farms. They want the girls here to go and work in the farmer's wife's kitchen. I want to keep them out of the kitchen. I think that you're worth far more and you've got a contribution to make. You've got to be new people in the new South Africa. I don't want you to be in the vineyards picking grapes. You've mastered mathematics and you know science so that you know what's going on in the world around you. I used to tell the girls in Afrikaans as well. I don't want you to go and work in Mrs. Van der Merwe's kitchen and become what the Afrikaners used to have a term for so-called colored girls—*meid*—which was a derogatory term. I said I want you to study, and I'm going to teach you to avoid that and to rise above that altogether. And I don't care what they have prescribed for you outside: at Livingstone we don't do what they prescribe. We do the things that we are supposed to. (Dudley Interview, 2003)

The message speaks to both the pedagogical and political responsibility of Livingstone as well as that of Dudley's students. What stands out throughout Dudley's career, whether at Livingstone, fellowship meetings, or other interactions, is that he is first and foremost a teacher. Even amidst protests, he always appeared as the teacher. Shortly after the Nationalist Party came to power, the government announced that segregation on trains, already the reality in most of the country, would be extended to Cape Town. There was also the beginning of talks to disenfranchise coloured men, and organizations on the left mobilized and announced a train boycott, with the soon-to-be dismantled Communist Party of South Africa taking the lead. The CPSA and NEUM clashed almost immediately, and the boycott, as well as appeals to overturn the legislation for segregated trains, was a failure. Teachers' Leaguers from Livingstone and other Cape Town schools, however, challenged the law. Dudley recalls leading student train sit-ins with other teachers, and he and Fataar were called to the Education Department because they refused to leave a whites-only train.

> We were summoned to the bloody Superintendent General of Education. They took us before the head of the provincial government. The head of the provincial government told us that we were servants of the provincial administration and that they expected us to devote all of our time to education. We said that in terms of the sort of conditions of service, we couldn't be in the service of the department

> twenty-four hours, but we were certainly teachers in their employ. And our job was to teach pupils, and we wanted these pupils to grow up with healthy attitudes. We wanted to train them for positions to take part in society, and we were not going to teach them anything which was injurious to their futures. We had the head of the government in a bit of a squeeze because of the fact that he couldn't challenge us on the question of our duty towards the pupils. We wanted, actually, to show that we were opposed to unjust laws that discriminated against people on the grounds of color. Then they came up with the "laws." We said that these are bad laws. So we were given a warning and asked not to repeat that sort of thing. But when we got outside the door we agreed they could go to hell. (Dudley Interview, 2003)

Dudley found it impossible not to teach even as he was being detained, and unfortunately for the next thirty years teaching and politics could not be separated in South Africa. There were teachers who did not step up to the plate and hid from political confrontation; their lives were good in relative terms. The conservative Cape Professional Teachers Association, that began with the split of the TLSA in 1944, was actually much larger than the TLSA. The continuing question, however, is how did the organization affect the children? In certain schools, among them Cressy, Trafalgar, South Peninsula, and of course Livingstone, they were not welcome. And the changes that came to Livingstone during the 1950s included a faculty that was more academic and much more radical in their politics. As 1956 approached and Dudley's term as interim principal was coming to a close, both his personal and public life again changed. At home Nerine's health was not as serious, and the Dudley's second child, Gary, was born. Richard Dudley, unsurprisingly, could not help but refer to their family planning as a Soviet-inspired five-year plan. At the same time, the Livingstone School Committee went to the superintendent general of education to ask him to appoint Dudley as the permanent principal of the school. This request would repeat itself on numerous occasions throughout Dudley's teaching career, but he was never appointed. The 1955 response probably should have been taken as a sign that Richard Dudley would never be the official principal of Livingstone High School.

> I was the best-qualified teacher then. By that time I had outgrown some of my feeble youth, and the teachers were prepared to back me up. I acted there for about two and a half years. Then when it came to making the position permanent, the school committee was called in by the superintendent general of education, Mr. Malan. And they insisted that I should be appointed permanently. Malan told the school committee this. I think it's almost word-for-word. He said to them, "Look, we know Mr. Dudley. We know that he's

> qualified for the position, but we also know that he has been fighting our policies all the time, and we are not going to pay him now for opposing our school policies." (Dudley Interview, 1999)

Ray Carlier was appointed principal, and the school became more academic and more political under her leadership. She stood up for both students and faculty, and Dudley's memories are of a school that was serious about the mission of educating and politicizing students under an oppressive and racist regime. Simon Banda, who would later become a teacher and then principal at Livingstone, was a student at the time. His memories of his education mirror Dudley's recollections:

> I think it was the recognition that every child has a potential for growth and therefore dignity, and this was something that was driven home to us repeatedly. The activities of the school weren't limited to mere academics, but were so broad so that you could find your place. That to us was very important. Just looking at the curriculum—it was so broad. Takes you into the natural sciences, the languages, the creative aspect was indeed there as well. The political issues of the day were integrated into the teaching as such, and so it wasn't academic work and politics as an aside, but it formed a unity in terms of history, in terms of geography, in terms of statistics in mathematics and so on. (Banda Interview, 2003)

Dudley and a handful of other teachers took on management responsibilities just as they had with Roberts, but they now had a great deal more experience. Although many of the teachers at the school were white, there was a Teachers' League ethos at the school that stressed hard work and standards along with political education and analysis. Most of the white teachers, unlike Humphries whom we met earlier, were not political at that time, but they were infused with the serious and hard-working ethos that was part of the TLSA tradition. Repression of black teachers had begun in earnest by 1955, and being a professional was somewhat of a shield from the Education Department.

> There were quite a number of white teachers on the staff, and we got along quite well. I think that they fell in with the sort of ethos that we were trying to create. The pupils were responding to the demands of the teachers. A number of the teachers on the staff were members of the Teachers' League, and the rule was you do your job. You are exposed to persecution by the department, but we are not going to be able to defend you if you haven't done your work, because if they come with the charge of neglect of duty against you, then there is no way in which we can defend you. (Dudley Interview, 2003)

Following the firings and subsequent bannings of African teachers, two coloured teachers met the same fate in 1956, and no one, the department included, could question their work as teachers. Willem van Schoor and Ben Kies, leaders in the Anti-CAD, NEUM, and TLSA, actively resisted the government and were vocal in both their criticism and socialist rhetoric. Kies has been introduced extensively throughout the text, but van Schoor was also a TLSA officer and one of the founders of the New Era Fellowship. As a lecturer at Sohnge Training College in Worcester, he politicized students and educated them in opposition to government-imposed "gutter education." Like his TLSA colleagues, he challenged the department position of a lesser education for black South Africans and taught his students to settle for nothing less than democracy and equality. Van Schoor is cited often for his 1951 Abrahamse Memorial Lecture, "The Origin and Development of Segregation in South Africa." Helen Kies describes and analyzes the firing and banning of both men within the context of politics, education, and apartheid:

> Their introduction of a system of separate education was a desperate measure to set the political clock back. There had been a growing unity among the oppressed by the time the National Party came to power in 1948. Well, they saw this as a threat to their rule. They had to devise a means of countering this growing unity, of destroying it. The most diabolical, you know, vicious aspect of their activities would be their control of education. It was to be a policy of retribalizing. Of pushing the oppressed back into their separate kraals. Of getting them to accept their differentness one from the other, and that their liberation could not come from unity among them. They were, as we said, going to "Bantuise," "Colouredise," and "Indianise" the various sections. The white section was, of course, superior intellectually and morally to all the other groups. For this analysis of the rulers' intentions in his presidential address, and for warning that the "Coloured" section would be next in line for the transfer of their education to a Coloured Affairs Department, Willem van Schoor fell foul of the Education Department's "misconduct" clauses. He was charged with "creating enmity between the races." Well, Ben was similarly charged for having published the Presidential Address in the *Educational Journal*. (Kies Interview, 1999)

While Dudley and colleagues at Livingstone continued to teach for democracy and against the government oppression that Helen Kies chronicles, he and his colleagues knew that they were also in jeopardy. Besides Jaffe, who only taught at Livingstone for a short time, Victor Wessels joined the faculty; he, Dudley, Fataar, and George Abrahams were known to the Education Department as very active opposition teachers and activists. That said, they got on with the work of the school trying to enhance the academic setting while teaching their students not to accept government segregationist educational policies that would soon be legislated and more viciously enforced.

The faculty worked at improving the library by providing students with books and publications that were not on the Education Department approved list of materials. Allie Fataar took the lead, but many teachers on the staff viewed it as a community effort with the goal of making the library the hub at the school. The faculty at Trafalgar had compiled a list of important books outside of the purview of the department that Livingstone used as a guide. Of course, Dudley and his colleagues in the Teachers' League read extensively. Besides the books cited previously, he was reading Tolstoy and Dostoyevsky at the time. The University of Cape Town donated books, as did foundations in the United States and United Kingdom. Newspapers were also part of the library, including *The Torch*, as were publications that teachers subscribed to and then donated. Dudley remembered the BBC publication *The Listener* as well as *The New Statesman* and *The Nation*. Besides providing different political views than the government reading list, the publications modeled a different writing style and tone.

It is important to understand that even in the 1950s, tasks like building the library, teaching the academic disciplines, bringing in alumni and other people to talk about occupational possibilities, providing college counseling, and of course political teachings were all taking place in a time that was already abnormal. Library books and publications had to be quickly hidden if an Education Department inspector made an unannounced visit to the school. And it was not uncommon for authorities to visit the school and question Carlier about teachers like Fataar, Abrahams, Wessels, Dudley, and soon Danny Jordaan and Neville Alexander, the former a member of the Fourth International and the latter a member of the TLSA and the Unity Movement, but also with much more militant leanings.

Ray Carlier was a member of the Teachers' League, and she stood up for the teachers on the staff. Officials would ask her to be vigilant and to report any misgivings or political activities, and her response was always that the teachers were hard working and cared about their students. The authorities had to know Carlier's affiliation with the TLSA, but one can only guess what they thought they might get her to say. In any case, she told the teachers of the visits to let them know that the Education Department and also the security wing of the government were monitoring their activities. Dudley and his colleagues were shaken by the van Schoor and Kies bannings, and they were well aware of the surveillance.

As Dudley often said, however, they had "taken a blood oath," and it was their responsibility and mission to continue teaching and working for a democratic South Africa. After the bannings, there was greater responsibility to lead conferences and meet with people in both the Western Cape and throughout the country to plan educational and political actions. Conferences were held during the school holidays, and trips were made to the

Eastern Cape and Johannesburg as well as towns throughout the province. The provincial meetings were usually TLSA Conferences where the discussion included both politics and teaching. Fataar would often speak forcefully about government oppression and impositions as well as teaching English. Other teachers would hold teaching seminars on various disciplines introducing new methodology. Outside of Cape Town, Victor Wessels and George Abrahams would often give political speeches in Afrikaans.

Clandestine meetings were held in townships in Johannesburg and other cities as well as in Langa at home. Dudley and his NEUM and TLSA comrades would visit at night because, as he says, "at night our tans would match anybody else's." By 1958 a great number of people from the ANC were banned, and young ANC leaders were in the midst of the treason trial from 1956 to 1961, so while there were risks the meetings in the townships were to plan political strategy against the apartheid regime. In both cities it was representatives of NEUM—Anti-CAD and AAC—who met and organized issues of *The Torch* as well as joint conferences. In Soweto the contacts were Tukewayo Route and Pumi Giyase, who were both writing on political development. Tabata initially made the contacts in Langa, but there was also the ongoing alliance between the TLSA and CATA. Of course, just a few years later everything moved underground as hundreds of people were banned, including Richard Dudley.

Schisms

In 1958 the Non-European Unity Movement experienced a schism, and of course if we review the great number of schisms on the left that we have reported in previous chapters, this should not come as a big surprise. The split ended up creating two separate divisions of the Unity Movement: one that was nominally led by Isaac Tabata and another by Hosea Jaffe. Dudley became aligned with the second group, and the story is unique from a research perspective because Allie Fataar and Richard Dudley have very different recollections and analyses. Fataar aligned with Tabata, although the depth of the alliances is not clear.

Allie Fataar and Dudley both remember the issue being land distribution, but again their descriptions and interpretations are very different. Fataar relates the issue to the Ten Point Programme and argues that just like the vote and education, ownership of land was to be no different for white people or black people. He explains that Jaffe's side did not want rural or urban blacks to own land because they saw it as becoming part of the capitalist class. Fataar's view was that there should never have been discrimination about what blacks and whites were allowed to do. The reality, though, was that the discussion was about Africans, not blacks in a more struggle or holistic way, and there had been great discrimination through legislation of peasant land reform that kept Africans from owning their own property. The Tabata camp viewed land ownership as essential and accused the other side of creating a false definition of 'capitalist exploitation.' Fataar explained that the issue was "how land, agriculture, and mining would be used in the interest of the landless population while bourgeois property rights were to be liquidated. Not the right to have large lands to exploit labour, but to have something to have some cattle and vegetables" (Fataar Interview, 2003). Fataar concludes with a declaration that the split was the end of the Unity Movement, but it also must be remembered that in a few short years apartheid oppression temporarily ended all movements, at least aboveground. Dudley paints a very different picture of the schism, although he too views it as the end of the AAC-NEUM alliance.

Dudley viewed the break-up from multiple perspectives. Initially, he had difficulty because he thought of Tabata as being a nationalist at the expense of a more studied analysis within an historical and anti-imperialist and anticapitalist context. He viewed this as a large difference in terms of both theory and political action. Disagreements did not have to be fatal and could even be healthy in the democratic struggle. For example, he believed that it was possible to work alongside the Fourth International even though they believed that the battle was urban and did not address the plight of peasantry in South Africa. Nonrecognition of the importance of international imperialism and capitalism's effect on South Africa was viewed as much more serious.

Dudley praises Tabata for his work with teachers in Langa and African farmers in both the Ciskei and Transkei. As to the split that led to the break, however, his memory is almost the opposite of Fataar. Dudley's memories are of a NEUM executive meeting where socialism on the land and the "Land and Liberty" slogan were affirmed as the official position of the organization. Tabata and others rejected the decision; the Non-European Unity Movement was no more.

While the explanations presented by both Fataar and Dudley might be essential to the Unity Movement split, after many, many hours of conversation with Richard Dudley, as well as a close reading of the thoughtful and detailed research recently presented by Ciraj Rasool in his dissertation, "The Individual, Auto/biography and History in South Africa," I have to question whether or not the land issue was primary or tangential to the split. Dudley criticizes ideology and politics without hesitation; on the other hand, he is not apt to disparage other individuals—remember the line "he had arms not wings" in his recollections of Ben Kies. On one occasion, however, Dudley did allude to Tabata liking personal acclaim, and that small assertion might better explain the 1958 schism. Might Hosea Jaffe have had similar needs of appreciation and power? Or was the issue at least partially about the Tabata-Jaffe feud that began in the early 1950s with discussions of the land issue, but also with accusations by each man against the other stating that they were each trying control the youth? (Rassool, 2004, Ch. 6)

The break is important for many reasons, and one relates to an ongoing critique of the Unity Movement being a coloured organization. Although Dudley and the TLSA were involved with teachers in Langa and CATA for many years after 1958, and the message of the Unity Movement in the Cape continued to include nonracialism, noncollaboration, and non-European unity; the day-to-day reality was that Dudley and his comrades taught in predominantly coloured schools, and their organizations were made up mostly of coloured South Africans. I will show throughout the rest of the book, however, that while the assertion is true, it is not necessarily a criticism. Whether or not NEUM should have been part of Congress in 1956 is an open question, and it is impossible to ascertain what may or may not have transpired in such an alliance. Within the context of the intensification of government repression of opposition activists—NEUM, ANC, communists and more—and the further segregationist legislation that included forced removals, the 1958 split partitioned the lives of opposition blacks, leaving TLSA teachers with universal opposition politics and local coloured activism in both the schools and the community. For Dudley and his comrades, there were continual changes—both horrors and resistance as Sharpeville approached. In 1959 the Dudley family completed their five-year plan with the birth of Russell. While the 1960s saw the continuation and intensification of Dudley's lifelong blending of teaching and politics, there were also heavy weights put upon the Dudley family and comrades when colleagues at Livingstone were arrested for their political activities, Dudley and other comrades were banned, and his parents and then his own family moved from their homes during apartheid forced removals—the legal racist action that is one of a number of experiences that haunts Richard Dudley to this day. These events and more are described and analyzed in the next chapter.

6

education for democracy II

From Bannings to Soweto

The first decade of apartheid came to a close as the South African government accelerated the pace of the separation of the races by "any means necessary." Besides the many racist laws, oppression included bannings, prison detention, violence, and murder. Dudley and his comrades in the Unity Movement and the Teachers' League were among the people targeted by the government. Although they were criticized at the time—and even more so during the struggle years—for being theorists rather than activists, they were vulnerable to firing and banning like the fifty-five African teachers as well as Ben Kies and Willem van Schoor. The treason trial of African National Congress leaders moved from the late 1950s to the first years of the 1960s, and the new decade began with the ultimate in government oppression, the Sharpeville Massacre. The event serves as a foreshadowing of government actions for the next twenty years and affected Richard Dudley both personally and politically.

In spite of the fact that the Unity Movement and African National Congress could not combine forces for true unity opposition, both organizations continued to fight against Bantu Education and other forms of apartheid oppression throughout the 1950s. At the end of the decade the ANC underwent another of the infamous opposition schisms. The formation of Congress in 1956 brought contestation between Africanists and multiculturalists in the organization. There were people in the ANC who did not like the influence of the Congress of Democrats or the Communist Party, or more bluntly, any whites. Led by Robert Sobukwe, a group broke away from the ANC in April 1959 and became the Pan African Congress (PAC).

Sobukwe was from the vast rural Karoo area of South Africa and was educated at Healdtown School before attending Fort Hare University, the same higher education institution that was attended by ANC leaders Nelson Mandela, Oliver Tambo, and Govan Mbeki. Sobukwe was an African languages instructor at the University of Witwaterstrand when he helped start PAC at a time when African independence was taking shape throughout the continent. In fact, when PAC was launched, congratulatory messages came from Kwame Nkrumah and Sekou Toure, the Pan Africanist leaders of the new independent nations of Ghana and Guinea.

At this point it is important to understand that although PAC was an Africanist breakaway from the ANC, the racial identity of the organization is much more complex than the apartheid-era racial distinctions of 'African,' 'coloured,' 'Indian,' and 'white.' PAC did follow the wave of African independence—Africa ruled by Africans—but the definitions have both breadth and depth. Early on coloureds and Indians were members of the Pan African Congress, and in individual lives there was the inclusion of progressive white South Africans. PAC had more contact with the nonracial NEUM then it had with the ANC, opposition politics and racial distinctions are not easy. Consider the example of Sedick Isaacs who spent thirteen years at Robben Island Prison because of his political activities:

> The Pan Africanists had just slipped away from the African National Congress in '59, and they were more energetic, more radical. And I was also energetic and radical, and I thought that would be a good organization for me. I became very much involved with it at the time. I ended up even making explosives. I got caught doing that. We went out to the rural area to test it. We were driving back and one of my friends stopped, and just when he stopped the police picked us up. I think they were watching. I had a girlfriend who was white. The police were also watching me in terms of the Immorality Act. And I think that's partly why they might have been watching. (Isaac Interview, 1999)

In December 1959 both the ANC and PAC announced the beginning of antipass campaigns. PAC trumped the older organization by initiating its nationwide action on March 21, 1960. While both organizations wanted to fill the prisons with antipass protestors, the tone of the PAC initiative was less Gandhi-like and more confrontational (Dubow, 2000, p. 61). PAC distributed a leaflet that read: "If one man is arrested for not having a pass, you will stop there and then and tell the police you do not have passes either. Demand that they arrest you all. Go to gaol under the slogan 'no bail, no defense, no fine' " (Rive, 1964, p. 15).

One of the locations of the antipass campaign was Sharpeville, a town in the Vereeniging district south of Johannesburg. More than a thousand people marched on the Sharpeville police station, and for reasons unknown, the police opened fire, killing 69 people and injuring 180. Multiple sources reported that most of those hit were shot in the back (Dubow, 2000, p. 62; Ndlovu, 1998, p. 1998). In Cape Town, a student named Phillip Kgosana led protests at the Langa police station, and two people were killed. Work stay-aways were called throughout the country but were sustained only in Cape Town. Amidst a great deal of tension and reprisals, the police attacked Langa residents March 30 to end the boycott. The same day 30,000 people marched in protest to the Cape Town central police station and only dispersed when negotiations were promised. Of course, the government did not honor the word of the minister, and Kgosana was detained.

Richard Rive wrote about both the march and the aftermath in his novel, *Emergency*. Rive was a well-known Cape Town author who actually taught at Livingstone for a short time. He was born in District Six in 1930 and is featured as a friend and compatriot of artist and one-time Livingstone student Peter Clarke and poet James Mathews in *More Than Brothers*, a tribute to Clarke and Mathews. *Emergency* is set in a three-day period just after Sharpeville and told through a fictional teacher named Andrew Dreyer who struggles along with friends and comrades regarding their roles at the time. We meet Dreyer as he runs from police charging at protesters swinging their batons.

> What a bloody day. . . . The curt order to disperse. The look on the face of the police officer. The sudden electricity in the atmosphere. . . . And before he knew what had happened people around him were running, struggling, shouting hysterically. A woman stumbled and fell. A newspaper-boy ran holding his bleeding head. Andrew found himself darting between the stalls, dodging the police and the crowd. (Rive, 1964, pp. 21, 22)

The Sharpeville Massacre quickly became news throughout the country and the world. South Africa was condemned by the United Nations, and there were international threats of economic reprisals. Unfazed, the Nationalist Party called a state of emergency suspending legal rights and quickly moved to ban both the African National Congress and the Pan African Congress. Individual members of the Non-European Unity Movement, including Richard Dudley, but not the organization itself, were also banned in the next few years, and more than 20,000 people were arrested in the immediate aftermath of the massacre. The ANC and PAC went underground, and both organizations asserted the need for armed struggle against the apartheid regime. The former initiated Umkhonto we Sizwe (Spear of the Nation), referred to as 'MK,' as their underground army, and Oliver Tambo left the country to set up the ANC in exile. After Sharpeville, the most visible portrait of apartheid oppression in the 1960s was the Rivonia Trial, where

Nelson Mandela and ten comrades were brought to docket in 1964. Glenn Frankel describes prosecutor Percy Yutar outlining the charges in his book *Rivonia's Children*:

> He handed in the indictment and annex. For the first time the defendants received a copy of the charges against them. The state alleged that the defendants, "acting in concert and conspiring and making common purpose" with seventy named co-conspirators, the ANC and the Communist Party, had "incited, instigated, commanded, aided, advised, encouraged or procured other persons to commit the wrongful and willful acts of sabotage, preparatory to and in facilitation of guerrilla warfare in the Republic of South Africa, coupled with an armed invasion and violent revolution." (Frankel, 1999, p. 185)

Although the defendants were represented by three of the country's leading attorneys—George Bizos, Arthur Chaskalson, and Bram Fischer—after eleven months of trial and a United Nations declaration asking the South African government to end the proceedings and declare amnesty for the defendants, all of the men charged, with the exception of Rusty Bernstein, were found guilty. This was the world that Richard Dudley lived and taught in during apartheid.

Dudley and his fellow teachers continued the mission of Livingstone High School and the Teachers' League of South Africa in the 1960s, stressing the importance of education in correspondence with an understanding and commitment to equality and democracy in South Africa. Ironically, the split in the Non-European Unity Movement was finalized in 1961 when Isaac Tabata launched the African People's Democratic Union of South Africa (APDUSA). Tabata asserted that the organization would promote the Ten Point Programme and act as the "military and political" arm of NEUM. Maurice Hommel argues that Tabata and comrades believed that NEUM was too teacher-centered to act on the Ten Point Programme, thus the need for APDUSA. It is not a clear argument, however, and is not contextualized through the Tabata-Jaffe feud. Tabata made a strong distinction between "teachers with the fighting spirit" and "quislings" in "Boycott as a Weapon of Struggle," and Teachers' Leaguers joined him in APDUSA. For Dudley and other members of the TLSA, the job was to provide a normal and exemplary academic education while at the same time helping their students to critically analyze and challenge the colonialist, capitalist, and racist realities of South African apartheid. Malcolm Campbell is a well-known architect in Cape Town who attended Livingstone at the time:

> It was during my stay at the school that I was initiated to politics. It was done very subtly in the classroom with teachers like Dudley and Mrs. Petersen raising social issues, but also the school had a reputa-

> tion as a political school, and one expected people like Dudley to talk about political issues. He never gave political speeches, but he made people understand and realize there were more important things out there then the purely academic. (Campbell Interview, 2003)

Dudley's life exhibited little separation of personal from public because family, school, and politics were continually crossing paths. For example, just before the Group Areas Act directly affected his father and mother when the government forced them to sell their Palmboom Road home in 1961, Dudley involved them in resistance politics. They helped hide Bongalizwe Joyi, a resistance activist. Dudley recalls:

> He was an extraordinary individual, a very powerful personality. We were at that time under the Verwoerdian laws, banning meetings and so on. We had a secret meeting in Garth Avenue in Athlone. Top people in the AntiCad movement and the Unity Movement met there. And there was a knock at the door. We had people outside, of course, who were our eyes and ears; they knew this individual and they reckoned that they were free to tell him where we were. And when Cobus went to the door who should turn up here but this fellow. I think Cobus nearly fell over. Four of us were given a secret mission to find a safe haven for him. We were not to speak to anybody but the other three in our group. We had to find a safe haven and we chose my father's place. That was just before the Group Areas Act was enforced. My mother by that stage had become ill, but they were prepared to accept this chap and they looked after him. It was absolutely secret. I had to transport him at night into the townships where he met his people, under the condition that he didn't tell them who I was. They provided him with the necessary funds because his plan was to get to Lesotho and then to make his way into the Transkei at nighttime to continue the struggle. The chap had enormous guts and courage! And then when his time was up, we had to arrange for him to get out of here. And that is also quite interesting. I had a 1942 Chevrolet which I think by that time must have been associated with my name. So a question arose as to how we were going to get out. The Civil Rights League made arrangements for him to escape. They made arrangements for him to be picked up on the outskirts of Bellville so they could get on to the National Road. So what I did was I let my brother-in-law have my Chevrolet, and I took his Morris Oxford, which was a different colour as well. And then I transported this chap to the meeting point. We met Patrick Duncan—Liberal Party, son of the one-time governor general. So he arranged for the train tickets through to Lesotho, and he succeeded getting him out of the country. (Dudley Interview, 2001)

As Dudley did his work at Livingstone High School and in the Teachers' League of South Africa in the 1960s and 1970s, government oppression was ever-present. Forced removals, teacher imprisonments, and bannings came on quickly after the Sharpeville Massacre. Soon after Samuel and Alleta Dudley helped Bongalizwe Joyi, Alleta died. Richard Dudley is convinced that her illness was connected to knowing that she was going to be forced by the government to leave the house that she had lived in her entire adult life, the home where she raised her children and lived comfortably with a community of family and neighbors. The Group Areas Act was first passed in 1950 with the purpose of bringing total racial uniformity to residential areas. Although Sophiatown in Johannesburg and District Six in Cape Town are the areas known throughout the world for South African government forced removals, the Nationalist Party actually started enforcement in the late 1950s and Cape Town was hit very hard. Families were notified that they were no longer allowed to live in their homes, and the railroad lines were used as markers to designate white and black neighborhoods. Between the 1950s and the 1980s over 150,000 black Capetonians were forcefully removed from their homes.

Samuel Dudley was paid R6,200 ($1000 today) for his home, and like many other homes in the area, it was then revalued at R40,000. The house is probably worth three or four million rand today. Richard Dudley is still very emotional when he speaks of his parents having to leave the family home.

> Anyhow that was the last thing that my father did in South Africa—provide a safe haven. And shortly after that the axe fell on him, and he had to surrender that place. Got something like R6,200 because it was a forced sale. It was an eight-room house with kitchen and bathroom standing on half an acre. And today it's valued, the ground itself is valued at something like about a million rand (actually much more). They call that the millionaires mile now. It's quite ridiculous because my father got 6,200 rand for that. When that axe fell, my mother died and my father's spirit was broken, and he and my mother had arranged to go and spend their wedding celebration overseas with my brother. When that happened, my mother of course died, the heart. My father then was told he had to move out of there, and they wanted to give him a bare piece of ground down on the Cape Flats. It was no more than bush. (Dudley Interview, 2001)

Samuel Dudley moved to England where he lived with his eldest son in Essex. Soon the rest of the family, with the exception of Richard Dudley, joined their father and brother as expatriates. Of course they were not alone, as many black—mostly coloured—South Africans emigrated at the time and throughout the apartheid years. Dudley is greatly saddened by what the government did to his family, to other people, and even to institutions like St. Andrew's Mission School; yet he is philosophical about South Africans who left the country. One of the commonplaces amongst TLSA comrades was a condemnation of people who left and moved to the United Kingdom, Australia, New Zealand, Canada, or the United States. The expatriates were not viewed as traitors but close to it. Condemnation is somewhat contradictory because everyone had family and friends who left. Richard Dudley and I spoke about how some people struggled deeply with whether to go or stay, and that other people would have surely been incarcerated if they had not run. While Dudley did not think of leaving, he is insightful on the issue. "I was totally committed here in the work that I was doing. I don't think that I ever gave serious thought to that. We took blood oaths, you see. I looked at it in this way. Some people would have been destroyed if they had stayed here. And there were others who had the ability to survive here." (Dudley Interview, 2001)

The Group Areas Act would personally hit Dudley again in the early 1970s when he and his neighbors were notified that Claremont was designated as a "white-only" district. A colleague at Livingstone had suggested buying a lot to build on in Elfindale, and although it was pretty much bush at the time, Dudley bought the property that he still lives on today for R2,000. It should be noted that because of his political activities, including his banning that we will discuss below, the house was bought in Iris Dudley's name. In 1973 when the Dudleys and their neighbors were forced to leave York Street, the Elfindale house was built with the help of friends, comrades, and colleagues. To this day there are still artisans and others who make frequent stops to check up on the Dudleys, and small produce sellers often interrupt our interviews with gifts. When the Dudleys were forced to move, Nerine was a medical student at UCT, Gary was in his last years at Livingstone, and Russell was four years behind Gary.

> When we moved in here, my wife and I were at an advantage because of the fact that a number of the people living here were ex-pupils of mine. But my children were hopelessly lost because they had to reestablish the kind of links that they had when they were in Claremont. We used to have to take them for the first few years from here through to Claremont to renew those contacts. (Dudley Interview, 2002)

While neither Iris nor Russell Dudley spoke much about the move to Elfindale, Gary Dudley dealt with the move within the complexity of his place in the Dudley family. While he was taught politics when he was nursery school age, he constantly shunned involvement with his parents' political associates and the youth political organizations. Instead, he found life with his friends in the neighborhood and through sport, mostly soccer. He does remember his father being away quite often; the nursery school age political teaching had to do with his parents teaching him that the government was bad and the police were not their friends. He laughs as he remembers making the point with other three-year-olds. His life was somewhat rebellious as he experimented with friends as a teen, and his devotion to sport was the antithesis of his father's political involvement. He did well at school, but his favorite teacher was John Burch, the physical education instructor. At the time of the move to Elfindale, Gary had created his life around friends and sport rather than the model of his father, who was a schoolmaster and politico. Thus the move to Elfindale had different meanings for Gary and Richard. He made it back to see his friends, but being separated allowed him the distance to hone his sport, an escape from the politics that always hovered not only at Livingstone but also on York Street.

Between the time when Dudley's parents and his own family were removed from their homes due to the Group Areas Act, much happened to him and his comrades at Livingstone High School. Dudley and many other teachers were banned, including his Livingstone colleagues, Allie Fataar, George Abrahams, and Victor Wessels. Other teachers at the school, such as Neville Alexander, were detained, and some, such as Kenny Jordaan and Allie Fataar, escaped the country to avoid imprisonment. In addition, Dudley and his teaching colleagues had to keep the school afloat amidst the imposition of incompetent and sometimes corrupt principals who were assigned to the school by the state. Dudley was banned along with more than 200 other black teachers in 1961 after the government action against the ANC and PAC following the bannings of fifty-five African teachers as well as Dudley's comrades Ben Kies and Willem van Schoor in the 1950s. Beginning in 1956 the police often visited both Dudley's home and Livingstone to monitor his actions. As we explained in the preceding chapter, Ray Carlier often informed Dudley of the Livingstone visits. Iris Dudley refused to allow the police to enter their York Street home and told them that they were well aware that he was at his teaching post at Livingstone. The police would also go to his parents home, and his mother would tell them that he had not lived in the house for many years—no more, no less. Visiting both Iris and his parents was a particularly insidious type of intimidation that was practiced throughout the struggle years in an attempt to raise fear and embarrassment among activists' families. In Dudley's case, however, it was almost as if he expected to be banned.

When security police did come to the school with banning orders, Ray Carlier called Dudley, Fataar, Abrahams, and Wessels to her office as she was ordered to do. She was extremely upset personally, politically, and also practically, as she relied heavily on the experience and expertise of all four teachers and feared what might become of the school. Although the banning was much more serious than the train incident of the early 1950s, Dudley and his comrades again saw it as an opportunity to challenge authorities who served the papers. The teachers were asked to sign the banning orders that accused them of being a "danger to the state," and they responded with a brief political lesson.

> We challenged them, and these blokes didn't like us when we belittled them, the security police. They weren't always articulate, and they weren't always literate. We took advantage of that sort of thing because, I don't know whether we were being unfair, and so on, but our education at least gave us an opportunity to pull their legs. And we said, "Look here. You know from all the meetings that you attended that we want to establish a democracy in this country." I remember telling them, the chaps that were there, because they always sent two, you see, it was a question of witness, on occasions like that. I said, "We also assured you that when we take over this country, we'll give you chaps decent jobs, so that you don't have to hunt down human beings." (Dudley Interview, 2003)

When Kies and van Schoor were banned in the 1950s, Dudley and his comrades viewed it as a strong blow because both men worked hard as teachers and in the fight for democracy in South Africa. Dudley was clear that the government's purpose was "to cut off the heads of the people who were the propagators of ideas, the organizers" (Dudley Interview, 2003). Dudley and his three banned comrades were all active participants in both NEUM and the TLSA, and they each brought specific skills to the organizations. For example, Fataar was known for his political teachings, and Wessels and Abrahams were especially respected for their ability, along with Hosea Jaffe, to influence rural teachers through meetings and powerful speeches in Afrikaans. Dudley wrote editorials in both the *Educational Journal* and *The Torch* and was also the secretary of the TLSA. Like the other teachers who were banned, he spent a great deal of time teaching politics to teachers and students in Cape Town, other towns in the Cape, and to a lesser extent in Durban and Johannesburg. This all came to an end, at least overtly, when banning orders were served in 1961.

Unlike Kies, van Schoor, and other teachers in the 1950s, Dudley and his comrades were allowed to continue teaching at Livingstone, much to the relief of Ray Carlier, but their lives were greatly changed. They were no longer permitted to attend meetings or participate overtly in NEUM or TLSA activities. Dudley was forced to formally resign from the Teachers' League and was also banned from his part-time teaching at the "coloured" technical school where he had taught for six years to earn extra income. As he put it, "one of my closest associates was poverty," and the money helped the family budget. The job enabled him to meet students who apprenticed or worked in the trades and opened up contact with the unions and working-class people. Dudley assumes that he was barred from teaching because of the contact with union people. On the other hand, it might have been "that they just wanted to, pardon me, bugger me around."

Dudley challenged losing his job at the technical school and went through the legal appeal process. Eventually in 1963, through the legal aide of one of Cape Town's leading advocates, Graham Duncan, he won the appeal. Dudley never returned to the position because he had already begun a degree in business administration at the University of Cape Town. When he and his comrades were banned in 1961, Wessels and Dudley decided to pursue degrees in law. Because of a loophole in the apartheid legislation, blacks who had graduated from a university were allowed to attend the institution at any time.

> Victor Wessels and myself were very close. We decided that we would actually prepare for the day when we were kicked out of the school. In 1963 we decided that we would assert the right that the two of us had to attend the University of Cape Town without getting permission from the Minister of Education, despite the fact that I was still under a ban at the time. As members of the convocation at the University of Cape Town, we were legally entitled to be part of the University. So we agreed that we would take up law. I couldn't fit myself into the kind of catholicism that is law. I went off in the direction of commerce. I decided to do studies in economic history. I got the B. Com. Degree, yes, after four years of study there. (Dudley Interview, 2005)

Dudley and Wessels knew the story of Ben Kies all too well, thus their motivation for further education. Although they were allowed to continue teaching and attend UCT, being banned from political organizations was a major life change. Dudley and other teachers who were leaders in NEUM and the TLSA did not, however, curtail their political activities, but rather went underground. They were very careful when they did meet comrades, and they provided their input through messengers as well as anonymous writings. Throughout the 1960s most of the political work went through the Teachers' League.

> I was the secretary of the Teachers' League at that time, and I got a note through the newspaper that I was to resign from all organizations. They listed those organizations and included the Unity Movement, the Anti-CAD, the Teachers' League of South Africa. I had to actually formally resign. I stayed away from meetings where there were large numbers of people, but we arranged to have meetings under the tightest security. Then we had couriers acting between ourselves and others. This included my two older children. I assisted in arranging certain meetings but I wasn't present. And

> then when it was necessary for me to provide them with anything else that was required, I used the children as couriers. I also had certain pupils at school whom I entrusted with necessary correspondence. (Dudley Interview, 2005)

Using children and students as political messengers in some ways muddles the Unity Movement postulate of fully understanding what you are fighting for politically and the later struggle years dictate of "education before liberation." In at least one case, a student that Dudley relied on became very much an activist in the early 1960s, long before the struggle years. Dudley and his TLSA comrades are ideologically clear when they distinguish between revolution and activism in the late 1970s and 1980s. Revolution comes with a deep understanding of the rightness of the time for change within an historical context. Student activism in the 1980s, and even more so the activism of people like Allen Boesak, are analyzed as emotional, reactive, and doomed to failure. Dudley may have been clear of the distinction at the time that he was banned, and he asserts the same criticism of activism that he and his comrades did twenty years later, but did he and his comrades nurture the activism they criticized when they used student messengers?

> There were pupils who felt that they could actually, under the circumstances that were developing, be able to deliver their own private blows against the state. Yes! As a matter of fact, there were people who fully believed when there was such a widespread demonstration against what had happened at Sharpeville and the bannings, that the revolution was around the corner. There were far fewer people in the 1960s, but even those few people believed that they could create the spark that would actually paralyze the ruling class in this country. Neville Andrews (a Livingstone student and one of Dudley's couriers) was one of those who was trailed. He was a very good pupil. He could write very well too, a very outgoing, sort of uninhibited individual. He too felt, you know, that this was the last moments of the NATs. People were looking for him. He escaped. Worst of all, he came to us for rescue. So we had to hide him. Then we got someone who had the necessary transport to pack him away. And he was ghosted into a safe area. (Dudley Interview, 2003)

Livingstone students joined students from other schools from the time of Sharpeville through 1994 to challenge the apartheid regime. In the early 1960s, the maintenance of academic excellence and critical politics was somewhat remarkable in light of the continuing chaos at the school within the context of the acceleration of apartheid oppression.

After the bannings in 1961 and throughout the decade, there was no rest in apartheid impositions at Livingstone High School. Ray Carlier's term as principal ended in 1962, and although that is itself an important and ongoing story, the next major apartheid imposition at the school was the arrest of teachers Reginald Francke, Leslie van Heyden, Kenny Jordaan, and Neville Alexander in 1963. It turned out that Francke had actually provided information to the state police that resulted in the arrests. Dudley viewed him as a "rebellious demagogue," not a revolutionary. Because he was a government snitch, Francke was released and returned as a teacher at Livingstone. He was shunned by teachers and students upon his return, and some of the art students posted cartoons that depicted Reginald Francke as a rat. Dudley did speak to him at the school and used the occasion as a lesson in politics and humanity.

> We were certainly not very happy about Francke. His membership, of course, in the Teachers' League was discontinued. But we tried to becalm the children without indicating that we regarded him as being innocent. He remained on the staff, and I was the only one who would assist him. The other teachers avoided him as much as possible. We had actually tried to get the pupils to understand that he was more a victim. (Dudley Interview, 2003)

Jordaan was a member of the socialist Fourth International and had broken with the TLSA in the early 1950s because he supported Edward Roberts in the Roberts-Fife fiasco. Jordaan was a history teacher, and he wrote political anti-apartheid articles that were subsequently anthologized by Maurice Hommel. The biggest loss for Livingstone, as well as anti-apartheid opposition, was Neville Alexander. Although he was a very young teacher in 1963, Alexander had already greatly affected Livingstone students, both academically and politically.

Alexander came to Cape Town from his Eastern Cape home in Cradock as a sixteen-year-old to enroll in the University of Cape Town. By 1957 he was certified as a teacher, had a Masters degree, and was on his way to Germany to pursue a Ph.D. His political commitment brought him back to Cape Town in 1962 after he considered academic positions throughout the world. "There was no way I was going to go anywhere but South Africa. Now let me put it this way: I think that my religious convictions, when I switched to Marxism/Socialism, sort of transferred themselves and I was deeply committed" (Alexander Interview, 1999). Because of his academic expertise, Alexander was offered a position teaching German at Livingstone, where he joined Dudley and others in 1962. He also was deeply involved in politics and broke away from the African People's Democratic Union of South Africa and launched the more militant Yui Chui Chan Club/National Liberation Front with Kenneth Abrahams, a Cape Town physician.

> We were already very critical of the TLSA as a political organization, not from the point of view of a professional organization. We always admired them for their professionalism and their dedication to pedagogy. But their political stance was so negative. We decided to go our own way and actually made up our minds to go for armed struggle after Sharpeville. And by '61 when I got back here, I was deeply into that sort of thinking, and I was very influenced by the Algerians as well as by the Cuban revolution. So we started organizing. And for the whole period I was at Livingstone, I was involved in underground work. I even organized some of the students as a site of our organization. (Alexander Interview, 1999)

Alexander left his mark on the school and had a great effect on students. He questioned both educational and political blueprints and brought youthful and avant-garde ideas to his history and German classes. Livingstone already had a reputation for teaching German, and having Alexander on the staff with a Ph.D. in the subject elevated the prestige. However, the thrust of his teaching was political. Students worked on what he calls "quasi-political" projects and did local oral histories. He wanted his students to become "militant activists."

> So, on the one hand we were extremely conventional in our manners, in our general demeanor, extremely conventional. We used to walk around with collar and tie. But on the other hand, we were really questioning. It was our way of operationalizing our left-wing ideology. . . . I didn't believe in blueprints at that time, you know. And I also think that's one of the reasons why children were very fond of people like myself and various others. The point is that we really gave them the freedom to explore things themselves. You need to take them further, and creating bridges has always been one of my main interests in life, actually, to see how people discover and then develop their talent. (Alexander Interview, 1999)

Dudley respected Alexander's teaching, and although they were not on the same page politically, they both believed in opposition politics and the fight for a socialist democracy in South Africa. "Well, I think my relationship with Neville Alexander was a very professional one. We worked together. We wanted to make a success of whatever we were doing there" (Dudley Interview, 2005). Linda Chisholm's critical yet compassionate article, "Education, Politics and Organisation: The Educational Traditions and Legacies of the Non-European Unity Movement 1943–86," is somewhat illuminating in that the only student comments are on Alexander and Dudley. An ex-student told Chisholm that "At school you were encouraged to be free, and when I looked at Dr. Alexander he was completely different to anybody I had ever seen. He was, he just looked so free" (p. 14). A second student, who attended Livingstone in 1976, the year of the Soweto uprising, spoke about Dudley. "When a guy like Dudley addressed the assembly, he was just a cut above everybody else you knew. He never spoke like ordinary people, for example, but he spoke in a way we dreamed we'd one day be able to speak" (Chisholm, 1991, p. 14).

When Alexander was arrested and then sentenced to what became twelve years on Robben Island, Livingstone students, including Dudley's daughter Nerine, who took German with Alexander, protested his detainment. Dudley and other teachers at the school advised the students on their planned stay-away.

> The immediate thing that happened was that the students arranged to have a protest by way of a stay-away that was arranged to take place for two days. The majority of the pupils stayed away. Remember that the protests against the Sharpeville shootings had certainly not subsided. What we do know is that those pupils whom we had cued up on the significance of the protest and what they needed to do had not to be thrown in at the deep end. We had to warn them of the degree of sophistication of the security police, yes. And so we also had to get them to choose the people with whom to work in the school. We would have known of their particular qualities and their degree of sophistication in matters like this. We did warn them that if they extended this stay-away that the ruling class wouldn't capitulate. They were demanding the return of those teachers. The teachers, themselves, issued a public statement deploring the arrest of their colleagues and calling for their immediate reinstatement. The Livingstone staff and Teachers' League. We did that despite the fact that that the Teachers' League was working under very, very heavy police surveillance. (Dudley Interview, 2003)

The police did come on the Livingstone campus at the time, and some students were arrested—a foreshadowing of the coming struggle years.

The Livingstone faculty was decimated even further in 1964 when long-time Livingstone teacher and political activist Allie Fataar went into exile, further diminishing the faculty. Fataar began his teaching in the late 1930s, and in spite of the fact that he was in exile from 1964 until the end of apartheid, he is still viewed as one of the foundational teachers of Livingstone High School. Arthur Hendricks attended Livingstone in the early 1940s, and he has great respect for Allie Fataar's teaching, referring to him as a mentor. Fataar taught English at the school and was known for his fiery politics but traditional teaching. In 2003 he spoke to his great-nephew Aslam Fataar and me about a typical pre-exile day.

> Now when we were in the Teachers' League and anti-CAD Unity movement, I was telling you that all of us worked 24 hours a day. I am studying through UNISA six subjects. So early in the morning you get up and make notes, you study and then have a meal, and off down the road to Livingstone and teach till 3 or 4, and then come home and there are political meetings, branch meetings right into the night, and there is writing to be done, then preparation for tomorrow's lessons and books to be marked. Weekends and all, you never have a minute. Weekends you are out to conferences and holidays out to regional conferences. There was no time for cinema, fun or games. This was done all the time. The teachers had education so it's correct that they should play the role they have been playing and still playing. They are part of the oppressed anyway. Anyhow I think the role is played by the teachers correctly. So that's the life we lived. (Fataar Interview, 2003)

Fataar escaped from South Africa in December 1964 after spending the day of his oldest son's graduation from medical school in an interrogation room. He left because he was certain that he was going to be charged under the Suppression of Communism Act and sent to Robben Island. He taught in Botswana, Zambia, and Zimbabwe during his years in exile, and he returned to South Africa in the 1990s. Fataar's departure from Livingstone brings us back to the end of Ray Carlier's term as principal and the stories of the faculty and students at the school.

When Carlier resigned as principal in 1962, the person who again deserved to be appointed was Frank Grammer. It became clear to the School Committee that the Education Department was not going to appoint Grammer, so they again pushed for Richard Dudley. The Education Department had different ideas and appointed a rural principal who never established himself at the school. The transfer of "coloured schools" to the new apartheid Coloured Affairs Department also occurred shortly after Carlier resigned. Both students and staff exhibited their commitment to nonracialism in defiance of the apartheid racial separation edicts. Amidst an acceleration of rules and regulations to further school apartheid, the government began strict enforcement of racially pure schools. There had always been a small number of African students at Livingstone; we noted earlier that one of Richard Dudley's classmates when he was a student at the school was Israel Kobus, the brother of his political comrade Cadoc Kobus. Livingstone had a strong reputation for both education and politics, and African students came from afar, sometimes outside of South Africa, to attend the school. Dudley's recollections and reflections of the time portray both the overt and covert nature of apartheid, but more importantly the nonracialism and resistance of students and teachers.

> They sent a message to all the so-called coloured schools that they were immediately to get rid of all the African pupils at the school. Now the principal who had been appointed in 1962 was one of their persons. He knew that if he made this public at the school that there would be a hell of a lot of trouble for him. So he attempted to get these children quietly off the school's premises, make them, as it were, disappear into thin air. But he was also dead scared of the authorities. So what he did was to go around to the classes and to tell the children that he wanted to see them with their books outside. And these children were sitting on the stoep outside the office and the classrooms. When our children moved from one class to another, they found some of their classmates sitting there. It became obvious as to what happened, and then these children mounted a strike—a stay-away in support of their fellow pupils—and demanded that they be reinstated. Now that, of course, was something that upset the authorities. Because here were so-called coloured pupils coming out in defense of the rights of African children. It was the very negation of what they had actually wanted. (Dudley Interview, 1999)

Dudley and other teachers advised the students and were actually quite proud of the action that was taken. And like some other schools, Livingstone was able to fudge the records so that these students, and other African students that followed them through the 1960s, were able to graduate from the school.

Unfortunately, Livingstone's next principal, Ronald Samuels, was even worse. Richard Dudley was the de facto principal in terms of nurturing both students and new faculty, and Victor Wessels was still an important teacher at the school. Ex-students as well as other teachers joined the staff, and a Livingstone education continued to combine pedagogy and politics. "I think that we were oddly bloody lucky because, by that time, a number of our ex-pupils had qualified, and they came to the school, and they proved to be very strong people" (Dudley Interview, 1999). Dudley also makes the point that bright and competent women joined the staff, as did Yusuf da Costa, a Unity Movement comrade who, like the Newmans and Arthur Reed, lived on the same York Street block. Dudley referred to York Street as an extension of Livingstone. During Samuels's reign as principal and through the 1970s, teachers pitched in to sustain and enhance both the academic and political life of Livingstone students. Although nonracial meetings and events were illegal, the school coordinated interschool activities, both academic and athletic, with schools attended by African students in Langa as well as schools attended by white students like the semi-elitist German school, Rondebosch Boys High School and Rustenberg Girls High School. The exchanges included sports such as cricket, tennis, chess, and soccer; Langa students also came to Livingstone for specific classes that were not offered at their school, and Livingstone students joined students at the German school for classes at both institutions. Jonathan Fry, who would later become a Livingstone teacher, remembered the exchange program:

> The black townships were no-go zones. If they caught you there without a pass you were in trouble. And we built up a massive relationship where we actually were in contact with black students already, and that was via Stella's pioneer club. She had a group of interested students who would forge cultural links with the students at Fezeka. So yes, that would sort of sensitise us to the plight of fellow students. And it probably made you far more appreciative of what you had. (Fry Interview, 2003)

Part of the motivation for the exchange programs was to bring together people who were legally divided by the state.

> We at that time were trying to defeat the kind of isolation of the schools by linking up with other schools. At that time too at the sports level, we used to try and defeat the state's purpose by having what we call triangular contests between the schools. It was difficult to get the white pupils to participate, but we did succeed in getting the African schools to send the athletes along. We'd mark out our postage stamp playground and they would have real contests. Then the state intervened. They told the inspectors who used to supervise things at Livingstone that in terms of the Group Areas Act it wasn't just a question of living in those areas that mattered, it wasn't just a question of trading in those areas; one of the key words in interpretation of the Act was *occupation* for use for which it was not intended. (Dudley Interview, 1999)

The exchange activities clearly relate to the nonracialism that was essential to the lives of Dudley and his comrades. In the mid-1960s amidst the great changes in South Africa and the imposition of apartheid on Livingstone, the school developed a school creed:

The School Creed

The following are the principles which constitute the Livingstone School Creed:

1. Equal respect for all people regardless of colour, creed or nation and an equal hatred for the beliefs that bring people of other colours or creed or nation into contempt.

2. Love for truth, learning and respect for the scholar and for all the means and instruments of spreading knowledge and culture and hatred for falsehood, ignorance and prejudice.
3. Love for work in all its useful forms and particularly for the work of learning; respect for all those who labour irrespective of whether the work be manual or non-manual and hatred for loafers and parasites.
4. Respect for the rights of others and especially in regard to facilities provided for the common use and enjoyment of all and hatred for vandals and bullies.
5. In all things to uphold the dignity of mankind and to abhor cruelty and injustice in all its forms.

The values articulated in the Livingstone School Creed correspond directly to both the academic and political tenets of the Teachers' League, the organization that Dudley belonged to for his entire professional life, as did most of the teachers at the school in the 1960s and 1970s. Noncollaboration and nonracialism, the foundational themes we have addressed throughout the book, are ever-present in the five principles of the Creed. The use of the word *hatred* projects a powerful statement towards both oppressors and quislings, but it is somewhat disconcerting. There is no question that Dudley was heavily involved in writing the document, but the hatred part does not sound like him. The Creed was launched in 1967 just before Victor Wessels was forced out of the school, and although I can only project, my interviews with other Livingstone teachers and Unity Movement comrades lead me to suggest that *hatred* might have been Victor Wessels's word. Dudley presented me with an annotated copy of the Livingstone School Creed when I first met him in 1999. His comments connected the Creed to the time that it was written:

> After the 1960–61 disturbances arising from the Sharpeville events and the conditions brought about by the banning of four teachers in 1961, the arrest of four teachers in December 1963 (the Neville Alexander group) and the uncertain conditions brought about by the appointment in 1963 by the authorities of their man as the principal, a number of teachers got together to examine the problems encountered by pupils and the staff, and to set up guidelines or principles according to which the aims of the institution could be driven and to provide an answer to the racist aims prescribed for different schools in the Christian National Education policies of the State. (Dudley, 1999)

The morning assemblies at Livingstone cited The Creed as Dudley and his colleagues taught lessons on academics, socialization, and politicization.

Faiza Bardien, who later became a teacher at the school, remembers political teachings from Wessels, Abrahams, and Petersen as well as Dudley. At different times of Dudley's tenure at the school he shared the platform with Edward Roberts, Frank Grammer, Allie Fataar, Victor Wessels, Hosea Jaffe, Neville Alexander, and Yusuf da Costa. During Samuels's years as principal in the 1960s, there were two assemblies—one that Samuels led that was religious and a second that was presented by Dudley and comrades. Samuels had left the Dutch Reformed Church and became a Seventh Day Adventist, and Dudley recalls that there were parental complaints at the time because of his proselytizing. This was just before Fataar went into exile, and he and Dudley tried to ease the conflict. Dudley remembers the situation with a chuckle, adding that at the time both he and Fataar were atheists.

There were much more important issues, however, about Samuels's honesty in his work at the school. He caused great damage when he had Victor Wessels banished to the rural town of Uppington. Dudley referred to the process as "Stellenbosching." Besides challenging Samuels on his fake degrees, Wessels, along with Dudley, stood up to him when he attacked their colleagues, English teacher Morgan Macarthur and biology teacher Stella Petersen. Both women had questioned Samuels about school finances. Subsequently, Samuels went to the Education Department and accused Wessels and Dudley of insubordination; there was a precedent in the early 1950s of sending political teachers to rural areas as a disciplinary action. While the department had no love for Dudley, he was the chair of the science department, and they knew that he actually did a great deal of the administrative work at the school. One can only surmise that they decided to placate Samuels, and of course they did not cry over sending Wessels away.

Samuels took a leave of absence in 1969 and ended up exiling the country to settle in the United States. Dudley's neighbor Arthur Reed was the interim principal until the job was filled by Robert Evans, who was principal of the school throughout the 1970s and 1980s. Dudley served as deputy principal and continued to hire and mentor faculty and enhance the academic and political ethos of the school by promoting equality, nonracialism, and academic standards in direct contrast to the mandates and goals of the apartheid government and the Coloured Affairs Department. He also had a hand in hiring and mentoring teachers during Evans's tenure at the school:

> We used to point out to people that, although the school now fell under the Coloured Affairs Department, the school had a set of aims, objectives, and directions which were very explicit. When I was given the opportunity of interviewing the teachers, we used to tell them what the school was all about. And we used to point out to them that we don't have Coloured children at this school; we don't have African children at this school; we don't have Indian children at this school; we have boys and girls. And if you can fit

> in with the program that we have, and if you feel that you have any prejudices and you can leave them outside at the gate of the school and so on, you'd be welcome. (Dudley Interview, 1999)

Evans came from Nelspruit in Mpumalanga, the northeastern section of South Africa, and although life there was very different than in Cape Town, he did speak English and had a degree in education. While Dudley and Evans did not always see eye-to-eye academically or politically, Evans supported the teachers at the school—a faculty that Dudley respected both as teachers and human beings.

> Make no mistake about it, the cooperation that we had from the staff was tremendous. And the school was one of the success stories. I think that we had developed an ethos and a coherence in what we were doing that enabled people to get down to the business of teaching, and I think that they did a damn good job. It wasn't a one-man band that was there. I mean I used to do a lot of the work, but my job, as I saw it, apart from teaching physical science, was to enable the other people to do the work that they were capable of, and they were very well qualified people. (Dudley Interview, 1999)

Dudley and Yusuf da Costa did much of the administration work at the school from the mid-1960s through the 1970s, and da Costa, who was Dudley's neighbor on York Street, viewed Richard Dudley as an elder and a mentor. Their work with students at the morning assemblies was especially important because Livingstone students were involved in political marches and placard demonstrations from the time of the Sharpeville Massacre through the struggle years, and Dudley and his colleagues wanted them to be aware of what they were fighting for as well as possible consequences. It was Dudley who hired his York Street neighbor, but he is quick to point out that da Costa was a thoughtful, experienced teacher. Dudley respected many of the teachers that joined the faculty at Livingstone from 1960 through 1980, but he speaks with special admiration for the late Harvey Hendricks and Yusuf da Costa. Because Dudley was so committed to the academic and political education of Livingstone students, he often tutored, mentored, encouraged, cajoled, and just plain taught his colleagues. His work day, including school and politics, left little time for relaxation or recreation, and he questions the lack of time he spent with his family because of his educational and political commitments. Dudley worked with the faculty, especially people that were new, to nurture an understanding of what it meant to be a teacher and to present the ethos of the school. As we noted in Chapter Four, as a schoolteacher he represented a curious combination of progressive pedagogy, rote learning, and strict discipline, including corporal punishment, although he argues, unlike some Livingstone students, that he often provided clemency.

"The only thing that used to get my bloody goat, and so on, was bad behavior. It did happen, yes. We used to use corporal punishment. I didn't like it. I always had suspended sentence. Yes, I used to speak to the pupils and point out to them that the school is here for everybody. You know, it's a question of having some sort of social conscience about things" (Dudley Interview, 2003).

Hard work, discipline, and resistance to apartheid education edicts such as racial separation and differential curriculums were all connected for Dudley and his Livingstone colleagues. I am again reminded of Linda Chisholm's criticism of Unity Movement schools and teachers for stressing an academic education that prepares students to enter the capitalist world. Dudley took direct issue with Chisholm's assessment and argued that the reason for high academic standards was because good schooling provided the weapons to fight the ruling class with equal skills. While I do not think it possible to prove either assertion, Dudley and his comrades are clear about their motives, and they truly believed that to insist on high standards was to challenge the apartheid state.

In the 1960s the government lowered the standards and lightened the math and science curriculum in white schools as academic performance declined and graduation rates dropped. Helen Kies explained that the government action was an attempt to hold up the face of white excellence in contrast to black inferiority. Dudley and his colleagues at Livingstone, Kies and her colleagues at Harold Cressy, and Teachers' Leaguers at Trafalger, South Peninsula, and other coloured schools took up the challenge. They pushed their students academically towards a university education. Teachers went far beyond the prescribed syllabus, and although inspectors objected to deviations or extensions to the state curriculum for coloured schools, Dudley and his comrades found ways to continue teaching to high standards, including both sophisticated learning and political awareness. Nonracialism also became part of the equation because they urged their students not to attend the new universities that the apartheid regime created to further separate the races. In Cape Town that would be the University of the Western Cape, a school that was established for coloured students and ironically became the "struggle" school after the Soweto uprising.

Dudley was joined by da Costa and most of the teachers on the staff in pushing students academically while still nurturing their political awareness from the 1960s right up to the mid-1970s when the government became even more oppressive—both in South African society and schools. It should be remembered that this was also the time when the Dudley family, like thousands of other black South Africans, was forced from its home. The intersections between school and home were many, as we have already noted. Among the neighbors forced to leave York Street were teachers at Livingstone including da Costa. The men knew each other through the Unity Movement and the TLSA but became closer when the da Costa family moved from Salt River in the early 1960s. During da Costa's ten years at the school, 1966 through 1975, Dudley taught da Costa administrative tasks and da Costa was grateful for his mentoring as well as his kindness as a neighbor. While da Costa knew Richard Dudley through the political organizations, when he joined the staff at Livingstone he was astounded by how important he was to the school.

> The dominant figures at the school at that time were Dudley and Victor Wessels. There is no doubt about that. Dudley the more dominant figure, right. I only became aware of it when I came to the school, when I saw the extent to which people would run to him for advice and all kinds of things during the day. I am talking about the teachers, including the principal. I don't think any decision was made at that school without his approval. He was also intellectually very dominant at the institution. He had a Masters degree in Science, one in Education, he had a B.Com, I think. And he could draw on this vast reservoir of academic work. He had also been very bright. There were very few things that he did not know about. He had this vast experience of being at the school for so long. And he was this dominant figure. (da Costa Interview, 2003)

The humanity that da Costa recognized is often mentioned by students, colleagues, and comrades and was present in both the school and community. For example, da Costa remembers both Richard and Iris Dudley coming to get his family for phone calls because the da Costas did not have a phone, and da Costa is forever grateful for Dudley's spirit at a time of family crisis.

> Look, I have a major philosophical disagreement with him today, because I am a Muslim and he is a Marxist. I will never forget what he did. And he took the time that day to be with me because of what I was going through. He took me to the hospital, brought me back, informed my brothers and sisters, and told me, if there is anything, just call me. That is the kind of humanity that I always tell people that although there were certain things that . . . people thought he was such a hard man. I mean even if the worst collaborationist walked into the school at Livingstone, he would talk to him. He was very different. He did not break personal relations with people because he differed from them politically. There was nothing like that with him. I called him Mr. Dudley. (da Costa Interview, 2003)

When da Costa left Livingstone after the 1975 school year and in the late 1970s and 1980s, he used his experiences at Livingstone to shape Steenberg High School. He hired some of his ex-Livingstone students as teachers and, in his own words, shaped the school in the image of Livingstone through much of what he learned from Richard Dudley at the school. At the time when da Costa left Livingstone to become a principal, the government was intense in the enforcement of segregation, but resistance was also becoming stronger and more overt. The next watershed, the Soweto uprising, for many scholars and activists marks the beginning of the "struggle" years that culminated in the end of the apartheid era. Students in the Johannesburg township of Soweto rose up against the imposition of Afrikaans as the language of school instruction. Ironically, Livingstone and other schools had been fighting the same mandate for over a decade.

Afrikaans was taught as a language at the school, just as German was. In fact, there were teachers who took their teaching of Afrikaans quite seriously, but they did not view it as the language of instruction for math, science, history, or any other subject. Tina Huller brought Afrikaans writers to the school and took students to theater productions. However, teachers and the school subverted the Education Department order to make Livingstone a dual-language school—English and Afrikaans. Dudley spoke about the issue and the school's actions:

> What they did actually was to appoint in the Cape Education Department a number of inspectors. These were white inspectors, again, pardon the term, but they were drawn from the contingent of experienced white teachers. And their task was actually to go through the schools and to see that the work was being done that was expected of the schools. But more than that, they had also to make quite sure that the majority of the people who were in the coloured schools were being taught through the Afrikaans-Medium. Now this language initiative of theirs was central to their application of the Christian National Education Policy. Because they believed, and they still believe of course, that particular section of the Afrikaner intellectuals, that language acts as the vehicle for people's culture, and so on. And if you wanted to nourish a culture amongst the so-called coloured section of the population which would produce an affinity with the culture of the Afrikaners, and in this way strengthen an alliance between the coloured people and the Afrikaner people, then language was going to be one of the most important weapons. Livingstone was a target because of the fact that the school was principally English-Medium. Let me put it this way, we dealt with this in ways in which the pupils could benefit. We used to simply tell the necessary lies about the home language of the pupils and the medium through which they had done their Standard Five studies, because our school, by that time started in Standard Six. We lied as effectively as possible to serve the pupils. (Dudley Interview, 1999)

Livingstone and other black schools continued to hold off the imposition of Afrikaans as a medium of instruction right up to Soweto. Besides hiding information from the Education Department, Dudley helped the faculty at Langa avoid teaching in Afrikaans by deluging the Natives Affairs Department with correspondence between 1974 and 1976.

Most important to Dudley, however, as 1976 approached was to continue to wed academics and politics at the school. It became harder and harder to convince teachers and students of the importance of thoughtful resistance as emphasized in the noncollaborationist and nonracial ideology of the TLSA, because the increased harshness of apartheid demanded action. Dudley and his comrades continued to urge thoughtful resistance and reminded their students of their privilege and the importance of using their "education for democracy."

7

education for (liberation) before education

Teaching and Politics in the Struggle Years

Much has been written about the 1976 Soweto uprising, where more than 15,000 students in Soweto, an African township in Johannesburg, protested against the government's imposing Afrikaans as the official school medium of instruction. At the conclusion of the last chapter we examined the resistance to Afrikaans by Dudley and his Livingstone colleagues, as well as by teachers at Langa High School. The difference at Soweto was that the police fired into the crowd and several students were killed; the numbers would multiply exponentially throughout the struggle years. One student, Hector Petersen, was seen in newspapers and television newscasts throughout the world as a fellow student carried his limp, dead body away from the police.

While there are multiple opinions on the impetus of the Soweto uprising—black consciousness, the African National Congress, student improvization—there is general consensus that the event marks the beginning of the struggle years that culminated in defeating apartheid. In addition, it is generally accepted that schools, through the actions of students and teachers, were one of the battlegrounds. Some scholars have overstated the importance of students in the struggle against apartheid. In spite of the policies of Reagan in the United States and Thatcher in the United Kingdom, disinvestment boycotts in the West grew from the mid-1970s through the 1980s; trade unions became more active beginning in the early 1970s, and the defeat of the South African army in Angola emboldened South African opposition both inside and outside the country. Still, school boycotts, placard demonstrations, and marches were part of the opposition, bringing great moral and tactical dilemmas for Dudley and his Teachers' League of South Africa comrades. While they continued to teach education for liberation, the prevailing mood of the day was the opposite: liberation before education.

Three South African scholars have studied the TLSA during the struggle years (Alexander 1989; Chisholm 1991; Nasson 1990). The great irony is that while Dudley and his comrades viewed much of the post-Soweto opposition as action for the sake of action, many Cape Town students and teachers who demonstrated and marched became members of the United Democratic Front (UDF) and the fledgling Western Cape Teachers Union (WECTU); most were educated politically by Teachers' Leaguers. Although activist teachers like Vivienne Carelse, Mandy Sanger, Glen van Hart, and others sometimes referred to Dudley and his comrades as "armchair politicians," they also spoke with respect of their TLSA roots and of their teachers as educators. Sanger attended South Peninsula High School, a TLSA stronghold, between 1976 and 1980; her activism began with environmentalism and moved to political action in her latter high school and college years. Thus she was taught by people like Dudley but became a leader in WECTU as a young teacher.

> They were largely Unity Movement teachers; they were opposed to what we were doing. They wanted us to behave very nicely and not spoil our chance of becoming doctors, lawyers, teachers. Their whole point was that you go to school and the best way to fight apartheid is if you are qualified. They were extremely anti-mass popular organizations. But they were role models in the sense that they were political. Yes, the fortunate thing about our school was that they would never be seen to be expelling or suspending students for being involved in politics; it was seen as a good thing. A lot of the teachers were members of the Unity Movement, so they'd invite us to the discussion groups on Saturdays and Sundays, and we'd go. They had an education foundation, but they essentially saw political action as being outside of school time. Despite my dislike and criticism of the Unity Movement, many of my teachers were inspiring classroom practitioners. They made school enjoyable and were committed teachers. Our opposition to the Unity Movement at school was not adversarial. It was more of a situation where as young students we resisted being politically adopted by them and developed our own independent political networks. (Sanger Interview, 1999)

Black Consciousness Movement, the Unity Movement, and Livingstone High School

South Peninsula, Harold Cressy, Trafalger, and Livingstone were similar schools, and students at each institution wanted to be included in anti-apartheid activism. As African students throughout the country were overtly challenging the Government, coloured students in Cape Town joined the struggle. Near the end of *Between the Wire and the Wall*, Gavin Lewis acknowledges the influence of the TLSA on student activists, but he also asserts quite strongly that the major influence on student activism was the Black Consciousness Movement (BCM) that came of age in South Africa in the early 1970s before the Soweto uprising. While the ANC is historically connected to Nelson Mandela and PAC to Robert Sobukwe, it is Steve Biko whom we remember when we speak of the Black Consciousness Movement. In the late 1960s Biko was a student at the black medical school of the University of Natal-Wentworth. He was a member of the National Union of South African Students (NUSAS), a predominantly white student organization that opposed apartheid. In 1969 Biko and other black members of NUSAS left to form the South African Students' Organization (SASO), the foundational body of black consciousness in South Africa. By the early 1970s the Black People's Convention was formed, and black consciousness was represented outside of the walls of academia. SASO published a policy manifesto in 1971 that defined black consciousness for South Africa, and Steve Biko wrote a descriptive definition in an essay titled "The Definition of Black Consciousness."

> Black Consciousness is in essence the realisation by the black man of the need to rally together with his brothers around the cause of their operation—the blackness of their skin—and to operate as a group in order to rid themselves of the shackles that bind them to perpetual servitude. It seeks to demonstrate the lie that black is an aberration from the "normal" which is white. It is a manifestation of a new realisation that by seeking to run away from themselves and to emulate the white man, blacks are insulting the intelligence of whoever created them black. . . . It seeks to infuse the black community with a new-found pride in themselves, their efforts, their value systems, their culture, their religion and their outlook to life. . . . Liberation therefore, is of paramount importance in the concept of Black Consciousness, for we cannot be conscious of ourselves and yet remain in bondage. We want to attain the envisioned self which is a free self. (Biko, 1971, p. 49)

Biko and his comrades believed that integrationist groups such as NUSAS, liberal white organizations, and political parties like Helen Suzman's Progressive Party were at the end of the day defined by white privilege; even when liberal white organizations overtly opposed apartheid, the goal was assimilation of black South Africans into the minority white world. Biko was also critical of the government homeland operations, as well as the tribal system that he viewed as an archaic means of oppression. In addition, the nonwhite universities and colleges were seen as institutions that trained black South Africans to police apartheid—colonials acting as colonialists. None of the above assertions appear to conflict with the tenets of the Unity Movement. However, the overlying belief of black consciousness directly contradicts nonracialism as a foundational personal and political belief. Biko's voice gained strength through the time of the Soweto uprising, and he and many of his comrades were banned, but not silenced, in 1973. Steve Biko was killed while under police guard in Port Elisabeth the year after Soweto. In their classic documentary history, *From Protest to Challenge*, Thomas Karis and Gail Gerhart debate the influence of the Black Consciousness Movement. They present a description of binary analysis that argues that BCM was an elite phenomenon versus the movement being the foundation of the struggle beginning with Soweto; BCM as weak organizationally versus the most successful attempt at popular mobilization; BCM as a small detour of ANC resistance versus the impetus of ANC revival; and BCM as part of apartheid racism versus a necessary resistance phase. (Karis and Gerhart, 1977, p. 90)

Karis and Gerhart maintain that there was continuing debate about the place of black consciousness after Biko's murder and into the struggle years. South African Marxists, for example, "dismissed black consciousness as hopelessly naïve about how to further the revolutionary cause" (Karis and Gerhart, 1977, p. 90). Dudley and his comrades would concur. The *Educational Journal* serialized a critical essay on black consciousness in the March, April/May, and June 1976 issues. "Black Consciousness: A Reactionary Tendency" was published under the pseudonym Mildred Poswa. The author was actually Neville Alexander, whose life we portrayed in Chapter Six, but as we will discuss below, Alexander disputes the version of the essay that the Teachers' League published. The article was reprinted in 1982 and is often referred to by Unity Movement people. It begins with a review of black consciousness in the United States as the origin of the South African movement. While Dubois and Malcolm X, the Student Nonviolent Coordinating Committee and Stokely Carmichael, the Black Panthers, Huey P. Newton, Eldridge Cleaver, and Bobby Seale were certainly known to the young SASO leaders, black consciousness in South Africa also had its origins in the work of Frantz Fanon, Julius Nyerere, Kwame Nkrumah, and Robert Sobukwe. Steve Biko is never mentioned by Alexander, and the article asserts that black consciousness played into oppression and power in both the United States and South Africa by tacitly promoting divide and rule. In addition, when discussing South Africa the article firmly assails the racialism of a black-only movement and connects the argument to a critique of BCM for ignoring the real cause of oppression in South Africa and throughout the world—imperialism and economic power.

Neville Alexander has told numerous people that the title of the article was supposed to include a question mark: "Black Consciousness: A Reactionary Tendency?" At various places in the text where issues were presented as statements, they were supposed to be in the form of questions. Earlier we discussed the collective publishing process of the *Educational Journal*. Remember, the procedure included comrades reading and critiquing and rewriting submitted articles. Alexander recollects discussions with both Victor Wessels and Helen Kies, but he does not recall viewing the article as it was finally published. In fact, his relationship with Wessels ended after he read the published version of "'Black Consciousness': A Reactionary Tendency."

What is more astounding to me than Unity Movement criticisms of BCM in the 1970s is that Unity Movement elders continue to be adamant in their analysis thirty years later. Dudley told me that there was a meeting between Victor Wessels and Steve Biko, but they could not come to an agreement that would have joined the organizations. It is almost as if Dudley has the article memorized, but on some issues, like conspiracy, he even goes beyond the article. For example, he makes the claim that Richard Nixon was a supporter of black consciousness in the United States because it helped divide the opposition. There are very few issues where our discussions, Dudley and mine, became a bit contested, but somehow I could not fathom Nixon and Stokely Carmichael on the same page. That said, Dudley's analysis of black consciousness in South Africa is quite reflective.

> To get people to understand the basis of nonracialism is far more difficult than to get them to latch onto something which is essentially emotional. It is a knee-jerk reaction to a situation like that in South Africa where you identify people as being white as being the source of all your problems. Our view was that you cannot look at things in terms just of colour in this country. The things which strike people immediately are the discriminations on the basis of colour between people, but the reasons for this kind of discrimination actually lie deeper than just questions of colour. We saw the fundamental reasons in the whole system of colonialism and in the history that went along with that. Because we also argued that the large number of problems in this country concern issues of colour and race, but the fundamental solutions to those problems cannot be pursued along lines of colour and race. There were economic issues and also sociological issues, and you would have to negate your racism. You'd have to negate your racialism and then place at the forefront of people's focus the fact that there is only one human race. So it meant, actually, that we had to step up our process of drawing people into the field of ideas and getting them to understand that what they had been lured into is actually going to be a dead end. That it's not going to lead to any kind of framework of ultimate solutions for this country. (Dudley Interview, 2003)

Certainly it is not surprising that the above analysis focuses on nonracialism, class, and power. In some ways black consciousness symbolizes the many changes that the struggle years brought to South African opposition politics that challenged the Unity Movement emphasis of education for liberation. For Dudley, just as in the 1960s, the personal and the public as well as the political and pedagogical were intimately intertwined. He had his first experience with heart problems, but it did not slow his pace at Livingstone or in the community, except for a 1977 trip to England and Canada to visit his sisters, whom he had not seen since 1963, and his brother, whom he had not seen since 1950. Dudley's father had died in 1976. The dilemma at the school was joining academic excellence with reasoned political awareness at a time when the public mantra was action and activism. Politically, Dudley and his comrades turned to community civic organizations as well as the growing nonracial sports movement.

The late 1970s and 1980s were difficult times at Livingstone. Dudley directly connected the black consciousness movement to student criticism and bad behavior toward white teachers as well as in-school protests against nonracial interschool programs that Livingstone had developed with white schools:

> The ones who wanted to display themselves publicly became the main spokespersons for "Black is Beautiful." They didn't know very much about Frantz Fanon, but they knew what Steve Biko had been saying. That in this way the black man has to establish himself, his dignity, and self-respect, and that he must speak up, and he must speak out. But very often they were keen to speak up and to speak out, but they didn't know what to speak. So a lot of the feeling turned against so-called whites at the school, despite the fact that the bona fides of the teachers there were, I think, impeccable. This just gave rise, I think, to quite a lot of difficulties. You had to take certain of these individuals aside to point out to them that this is not the sort of thing that you do when you claim that you are building upon dignity in order to remove the curse of racism in this country. And that you are sort of doing the self-same thing in reverse to what you claim people had done to rob you and the population of this country. I said, "That's not good enough. You've got to think your way past this." (Dudley Interview, 2003)

When Dudley speaks of students at Livingstone and the Black Consciousness Movement, one of the students he is speaking of specifically is Alan Liebenberg, a student at Livingstone in the 1970s who went on to be both a teacher and principal. Dudley seldom is harsh or total in his criticism of other human beings, but it is clear that he is not fond of Alan Liebenberg, mostly because he believes that Liebenberg was not thoughtful and acted unfairly towards white teachers at Livingstone. Liebenberg, in turn, believes that Dudley let him down when authorities came to arrest him at the school, and he remains very angry towards Richard Dudley and Livingstone High School. He is the only student, teacher, or political figure that I spoke with, whether they agreed or disagreed with Richard Dudley, who condemns him for his actions at the time. Liebenberg readily speaks about driving out white teachers. "And I think mischief was in the making because we gave them a hard time. I don't know whether it was racism in reverse, but we were reacting to those white people in the school. And so one after the other left. Some because of us giving them a hard time, and others because of their personal circumstances, but they didn't stay long" (Liebenberg Interview, 2003).

In retrospect, Dudley was saddened by the events, but it did not keep him from teaching and nurturing the academic and nonracial mission of the school. In addition, he got great satisfaction from the teachers and students who joined him in the charge. One particular student from the pre-Soweto years, Denise Simms, was very important to the school in terms of the nonracial mission. Dudley referred to her as "a sort of St. Joan." As a tenth grader Simms was elected to the Student Representative Council, and Dudley's recollection is that at that very young age she became the prominent student leader at Livingstone High School. Simms would go on to study at Harvard University and then return to South Africa as a professor at Rhodes University. Her mother had attended Livingstone and was political, and her stepfather was the president of the South African Council on Sport (SACOS), the nonracial sport organization that Dudley worked with beginning in the mid-1970s. Dudley is clearly taken by her strength as a young student.

> She decided that the Student Representative Council at the school had become somewhat flabby. We had enlarged the scope of teaching at the school and had a number of school societies which were very functional. There was a History and Debating Society. There was a Film Society. There was the Science Society. And then there was the Pioneer Society, which took the initiative in getting other schools working along with Livingstone, including the so-called established white schools. But when this Black Consciousness Movement came onto the scene, they wanted us actually to cut out all these associations with the so-called white schools. We had working relationships with the German School up there in Tamboerskloof and so on—very, very fruitful ones as well. And while there was a certain amount of sympathy that we had with the pupils who had been caught up in the Black Consciousness Movement, there was, in our view, a danger with this sort of thing taking over at a school. She was in Standard Eight. So that meant that she was about fifteen or sixteen years of age. The sad thing about it was that for the first time there was a conscious development of an attitude towards the white teachers at the school. So she got up there and took this creed

> that we had developed and pointed out to the children what they, in fact, should be doing if they were going to do justice to the role that the school had to play. (Dudley Interview, 2003)

Dudley also believed that Livingstone High School was fortunate because of the wave of caring, thoughtful, political, and hard-working teachers who joined the staff after the government raided the school in the 1960s, sending Alexander to jail, Fataar and Jordaan into exile, and Wessels to the countryside. He spoke with special admiration of John Burch, who took over physical education at the school in the 1960s, but even more so of the women who continued to teach at Livingstone through the 1970s and some into the 1980s. Tessa Fairbairn stood out as a giant, but Dudley also spoke with admiration of Pam Dewes and Pam Hicks. The respect is mutual, as all three teachers viewed Dudley as representative of Livingstone High School. Fairbairn reflected on Dudley:

> We always used to be surprised that he wasn't the headmaster until someone told us that he couldn't be headmaster because he is too politically involved. I think those values that R. O. had/has, he certainly still has them in a big way, permeated Livingstone in many ways. I see Mr. Dudley enormously as a man of huge wisdom, intellectual wisdom and integrity. Livingstone meant integrity. It meant dignity. It meant hope. It meant realizable dreams—nothing wishy-washy about Livingstone. Livingstone was a centre for excellence and it went out to achieve that. It attracted those children who wanted to go into the professions if possible. They didn't always get there, but that is what they wanted. It was a place of value, without doubt. But it was also a place of a huge amount of fun and a huge amount of laughter and a huge amount of challenge. Livingstone teachers made South Africa better. (Fairbairn Interview, 2003)

Dudley credited Fairbairn and later Dewes with reinvigorating the library, and he forged a relationship with Hicks partially because they were both in the sciences. Dudley and Hicks still communicate often and talk about family as well as educational issues. Dudley reflected on Tessa Fairbairn's work at Livingstone within the context of the changes at the school in the 1970s and the pressures from both the black consciousness mentality that came to the school and the government edict to remove white teachers from black schools. I have to think that there is some irony in the fact that Dudley was absent from Livingstone for six months in 1977, and that is when some white teachers left the school. A number of years later, after Dudley retired, Beth Mclagan, who taught English at Livingstone between

1983 and 1985 and then again in the 1990s, explained that there were rifts at the school:

> For the first two years I wasn't aware of any splits amongst the staff. The first time I became aware was eighty-five, my last year there. Eighty-five brought a lot of stuff out of the woodwork. Ja, incipient sort of racism against us. We had a temporary principal who was a pretty dodgy person. I don't know. We had been heard laughing apparently inappropriately at something. Which was not to do with being racist at all but was interpreted that way in the staff meetings. There were some splits as well between the Unity Movement and the ANC. And suddenly for me it was like something which had been overall warm and comforting and wonderful, started splitting a little bit. (Mclagan Interview, 1999)

The late 1970s and 1980s were exciting times in South Africa because people were making change possible. It is quite clear that Dudley and his comrades did not relish the possibilities. Remember, on more than one occasion Dudley spoke about the students and some teachers thinking that revolution was around the corner. And although Teachers' Leaguers still assert that the democratic revolution has yet to come, the end of apartheid is not to be taken lightly in terms of oppression versus freedom. From even before Soweto through the student marches and demonstrations of the struggle years of the 1980s, Dudley and his comrades were intent on connecting pedagogy and politics and keeping students in school. And they really believed, and still believe, that the students and some of their more activist teachers were naïve and participated in action for the sake of action. Dudley and his comrades Helen Kies and Tom Hanmer have similar reflections:

(1) Dudley

> And we indicated to them that there was no way they could, in a few days of struggle, achieve what they were demanding. That they would have a long career in front of them in which they would have to be involved in this sort of thing. Now that kind of education, I think, was very necessary for these pupils. Because one of the other things that they were attempting to do from outside was to get the pupils to leave the school and to join the army outside in exile. What we tried to get the pupils to do was to understand that this was just part of a total political struggle. We didn't want these pupils to lose the momentum of their studies. And then there was a reaction against this by certain pupils. You know that the revolution was around the corner. (Dudley Interview, 1999)

(2) Kies

> The other youngsters could predict to the month when the Nationalist government would be brought to its knees. They had all the steps and stages worked out. They thought it was just a matter, you know, of Step 1—Accomplish. Step 2—Accomplish. Step 3—Accomplish. Step 4—Revolution and Freedom. It was all so easy. Some of my politically brightest pupils laughed at the idea that there would have to be a set of political, economic, and social conditions in the country before revolution could even be thought of. Others were going to put their money on guerrilla warfare! (Kies Interview, 1999)

(3) Hanmer

> There was a great deal of radical thinking towards action. Very often the thinking was not very radical in terms of an understanding of where they were going. The action was always something physically active, you know, you've got to march somewhere, you've got to get people together, you've got to get them out of their classes and any institution that gave any impression that there was work going on, you'd have to disrupt that. You'd have to go into the school and disrupt classes. (Hanmer Interview, 1999)

Livingstone and the other Unity Movement schools, of course, were not immune to the activism of the time. Dudley and his comrades tried to engage their students with both a continuing belief in the importance of education and what they viewed as thoughtful, educated, and reflective politics—not action for action's sake. They politicized the student societies even more than before Soweto, showed controversial films, organized student political debates, and joined students at selected demonstrations.

> We had our program from the Unity Movement where we had ten basic fundamental demands. And people at that time were raising banners and we said that your banners must actually show not only that you understand what this is all about, but that you can state precisely in simple terms what your fundamental demands would be. So we used to teach the pupils there that your basic and fundamental demand is your demand for the franchise, and franchised people are the ones who can work inside a desegregated education system. And they could articulate this kind of thing. (Dudley Interview, 1999)

Dudley also reminded students that they were privileged and therefore had great responsibility because many black people could not attend high school.

"I think that we had impressed upon them right from the 1950s that our struggle in education was a struggle for democracy and this was education for democracy. (Dudley Interview, 1999)

Amongst other respectful criticisms of Unity Movement teachers, educational historian and Human Science Research Council researcher Linda Chisholm questions socialist educators emphasizing academics and professionalism. To be fair to Chisholm, she does quote students who flourished under the mentorship of Dudley and his comrades. Recall the student quotes in Chapter Six regarding Dudley and Alexander. The point, however, of socialists favoring the best and the brightest over common students connects to Chisholm's questioning the rhetoric of Ben Kies on the mission of the TLSA and her assertion that the Unity Movement did not connect to working people, the assumption being that the organization was elitist. Dudley takes great issue with Chisholm's argument. In a 2002 conversation with Crain Soudien and me, he emphasized that she is wrong in her analysis of both Kies and academic favoritism. For Dudley, stressing education corresponded to Lenin's conceptualization of revolution beginning with the middle class, and the stressing of academics was preparation for a class of professionals that would challenge the system in the name of democracy. Dare I add that Dudley's argument also connects to the foundational thinking of black consciousness in the United States, specifically the Stokely Carmichael and Charles Hamilton book, *Black Power*, where the authors claim that equality can only exist when people meet as equals, thus black professionalism is a necessary element for democracy. All of this, of course, is more theoretical and philosophical than it is a description of the time. I think Linda Chisholm's more important error, in terms of the Unity Movement and teachers like Richard Dudley, has to do with assertions of losing the students and influence during the struggle, but we will return to that particular issue in the final chapter.

Dudley and his comrades in the Unity Movement and colleagues at Livingstone High School had to work very hard in the late 1970s leading to 1980 to keep students involved in academic pursuits while nurturing meaningful political opposition to the apartheid regime. He often tells the story of an interdisciplinary program initiated by the physical education master Burch, using the soccer World Cup to interest students in language, geography, art, music, history, and politics. Besides classroom events, students would actually compete athletically, have assemblies, and parade around the grounds of the school. The parade replicated World Cup opening and closing ceremonies, with each class wearing traditional clothing and carrying state flags. Amidst the demonstrations and police actions in 1976, Dudley relays the story of the ceremonial parade:

> And in 1976 there were people who reported to the police that these children were being taught military marches, and so on. Yes. And the police actually came to the school to search the school.

> Now I happened to be in charge of the Standard Ten class. And these boys, you know in drawing lots, they had drawn the Soviet Union. Their banner showed the hammer and sickle, and then they translated socialism into it: "What's yours is mine, what's mine is yours." And that they confiscated. They kept that at the police station for two years. They ultimately returned it to the school. (Dudley Interview, 1999)

The real action, however, was on the other side of the school fence, and two events at the school stand out for Dudley before the 1980 school boycotts and the heating up of struggle politics. The first memory is of Ralph Freese leading fellow students in an anti-apartheid demonstration. The second incident is of student teachers from the University of the Western Cape attempting to control teaching and politics at Livingstone. Dudley worried greatly for the students, because when they did demonstrate outside of the protection of the school, they were sometimes beaten and detained. Government "state of emergency" was often in play, and that meant there were few rules that had to be followed regarding police action. Dudley articulated what he and his colleagues faced and what they tried to emphasize with their students:

> The students used to march around the school. What was also interesting about that is that there were some people who were opposed to the idea of having these banner marches around the school. They wanted the pupils to go out onto the street. And when the pupils themselves ventured to go out onto the street, the police really fired into them and that happened again in 1980 and again in 1985. And so we indicated to them that there was no way in which they could, in a few days of struggle, achieve what they were demanding. That they would have a long career in front of them in which they would have to be involved in this sort of thing. Now that kind of education, I think, is very necessary for these pupils. Because one of the other things that they were attempting to do from outside was to get the pupils to leave the school and to join the army outside in exile. And there were bomb scares against the school, because our school was not prepared to take the pupils on these marches and so on. We did participate in certain of the marches provided these things were properly organized, but not at random. (Dudley Interview, 1999)

Livingstone students protested in the streets and went to organized demonstrations at other schools more than Dudley likes to acknowledge. However, he and his colleagues were successful in helping students organize protest demonstrations and political awareness sessions within the school. The main student leader at Livingstone High School in 1976 was a young man named

Ralph Freese. He was followed in 1977 by Russell Dudley, and that is a story in itself. Ralph Freese came from a political family; his father had been a member of the Fourth International and Freese's politics were already eclectic when he came to Livingstone. He had been raised on political meetings and in spite of deep family connections to Livingstone, he initially attended South Peninsula High School. Extremely bored at the school, a chance meeting with Dudley at a grocery store facilitated Freese's transferring to Livingstone for his last two years of high school, where he studied science and became a student leader. He quickly became involved in student organizations and remembers the academic, communal nature of the school, where students helped fellow students and Dudley served as a political elder.

> Some of the students went outside and said we aren't going to classes; 70 percent of the school didn't go to class and were on the field and we had a debate about what to do. The debate was around Gabriel's and my somewhat different positions. Mine being more informed—Ronald just said we have to march off somewhere, I don't know where to or why. So we had this debate, and I think the reason I won was that I had a positional advantage, I took a stand. So what we did is we said we would organise ourselves and other schools and then determine a strategy of what to do. So we dispersed with about fifteen people remaining in a classroom, the teachers allowed us to do it. We set off to the high schools to call a big meeting. We agreed with Mr. Dudley that we would not tell anyone they had given us permission. Mr. Dudley never said don't do anything. Many people around seem to have a belief that he said "don't march," but he would say "what are you going to achieve?" We would have short, sharp debates, but he never used the power that he did have to stop us. He could have said you will be expelled or anything, but he didn't. Often some of the questions he would ask would help us shape the pamphlets we wrote or so on. At the time we probably wouldn't acknowledged it. (Freese Interview, 2003)

Ralph Freese still responds to the times with confidence and charisma. He remembers the event as a debate with Gabriel, student leaders making a decision to stand with other schools, and Dudley's intelligent and civil guidance. Dudley, of course, was clear on his politics, and his memories have more to do with protecting his students.

An important addition to the analysis, however, is prominent in the way Dudley lived in the world before, during, and after the struggle. Although there were certainly times at Livingstone that Dudley treated students in a manner they might not think civil, students, colleagues, comrades, and family almost unanimously attest to his appetite for discourse. He listened to others speak and he was willing to have dialogue even if a meeting of minds was impossible; he even continued to speak with Francke when almost everyone avoided the man following his giving evidence against Neville Alexander. Ralph Freese remembers that Dudley believed in educated interaction as the means to democracy. "It was his attitude to thinking that was at the heart of it. His commitment to thinking rigorously and debate, to understanding everything, that was the big thing with Dudley. We had lots of debates in class. The content and way he directed people was excellent, and I don't think anyone who had been through it wasn't positively affected in that way." (Freese Interview, 2003)

The second incident that affected Richard Dudley a great deal in 1976 happened when student teachers from the University of the Western Cape came to Livingstone High School and began to make demands regarding both pedagogy and politics. The same type of thing happened to his colleagues at other high schools throughout the struggle years. Dudley and other Unity Movement teachers had been very critical of UWC since its inception in 1960, and the school was referred to as a "bush college" in various *Educational Journal* articles. The views of Dudley and his comrades were directly connected to their foundational belief in nonracialism; at the time of the founding of the University, the Unity Movement correctly realized that the school was founded as an academic institution to divide and rule. The "Mildred Poswa" article discussed earlier criticizes the Black Consciousness Movement for accepting the divide-and-rule origins of the University of the Western Cape and other "bush" colleges. Specifically, the article attacks the collaboration of the "coloured" Vice Rector, David van der Ross, for collaborating with the government in support of a racialist South Africa (Poswa, 1976, p. 12).

The University of the Western Cape was definitely founded to advance South African racialism with whites ruling blacks. For example, in 1970 over 90 percent of the faculty was white and over 90 percent of the white faculty were Afrikaners. In addition, by creating a coloured university, the division of Africans, coloureds, Indians, and whites was further exacerbated. The Unity Movement is also correct in its assertion that the black consciousness movement found life at UWC. Karis and Gerhart describe a 1973 anti-apartheid student demonstration at UWC and assert that SASO was the major organizer (Karis and Gerhart, 1977, V5, p. 138). In addition, a few years later a student at the university, Henry Isaacs, was the national President of SASO. However, from 1976 onward student activism at UWC was broader and expanded far beyond black consciousness. So when Dudley was confronted by UWC students in 1976 regarding both pedagogy and politics, the conflict was fundamental to the schism described above—education for (liberation) before education.

> We had students coming in from the teacher training colleges and from the University of the Western Cape, coming along wanting to dictate to us what should be done. I was in the office at the time,

> so I used to tell these people, "Look, I'm in charge here. I'm not in charge on my own. I have a staff. But I'm telling you now that we don't allow other people to tell us what we've got to do at this school. So if you've come for that purpose now, you must leave immediately." I said, "We're prepared to discuss it with you, but you must not tell us what to do." They would march out. And then we also refused them permission to continue practicing at the school there. By that time I think I had developed a bit of an elephant hide against this type of thing. I wasn't obnoxious in my attitude towards people, but I used to simply tell them that there was no other way in which we worked. (Dudley Interview, 1999)

Student action and Unity Movement criticism would continue in Cape Town and schools like Livingstone throughout the struggle years. Whatever the origins and stated purposes of the University of the Western Cape and other "bush" colleges, the reality in terms of the politicizing of young black South Africans was something very different. UWC, whether ironic or not, became one of the training grounds for the struggle against apartheid. While Dudley and his comrades are still critical of the de jure segregation of UWC and what they would call the present de facto separation at the university, many students who attended the University of the Western Cape during the struggle years viewed the school as the place where they were politicized in struggle activism. UWC students who studied at Cape Town high schools under Unity Movement teachers used the political education they received from Dudley and his comrades to analyze the racism that existed in both society and the university. They also decided to take the battle to the streets; although probably a simplistic analysis, this partially corresponded to their political education at the University of the Western Cape. Mandy Sanger was clear in her analysis of racism at the University, but she also spoke of how students responded:

> It was Afrikaner lecturers, they only spoke Afrikaans. They were incredibly hostile, so it was a very hostile environment in eighty-one. Yes, that was one of the reasons why we went there. Because we felt that it was an important way to organize students . . . I did anthropology but then eventually we had to drop out. We dropped out because what they taught was racist anthropology. I mean the moment you came with anything different, you were literally alienated or kicked out, it was very hostile lecturing. When we launched the History Society at UWC, it was banned from campus. It was a fight, it was a struggle to actually get it to operate. So even though I didn't do history, we all became part of the History Society, because it was the alternative to the SRC which we could not have. (Sanger Interview, 1999)

Many of the teachers I interviewed who came of age during the struggle spoke of becoming politicized at the University. Kevin Wildschut's recollections are representative:

> UWC was much smaller then, so you knew everybody and there was a sense of cohesion amongst the learners. Most of them came from a Coloured community. People who were ultra-conservatives, not actively involved in resistance politics, became more conscientized by what they saw on campus. By that I mean they experienced the beatings. They experienced the attacks by the security forces. They experienced the exposing of spies. They experienced the tear gas in the corridors. In fact, UWC was a radicalizing place. If you weren't an activist before you got there, by the time you left you sure were an activist! (Wildschut Interview, 1999)

As 1980 and more intense student protests approached, Dudley and his comrades were in a losing battle in terms of education for liberation. Mandy Sanger's words that were presented earlier succinctly portray the time. "Our opposition to the Unity Movement at school was not adversarial. It was more of a situation where as young students we resisted being politically adopted by them and developed our own independent political networks" (Sanger Interview, 1999). Not surprisingly, Dudley's younger son, Russell, who followed Ralph Freese as one of the student leaders at Livingstone in 1977, pondered his own place within the struggle. Unlike his older brother Gary, Russell was politically active, but it appears from his own recollections and reflections that his life is a continual search. At various times during the many hours I have spent with Richard Dudley, he has referred to the difficulty both his politics and position at Livingstone High School created for his children. We have already discussed Gary Dudley's apolitical views and life as a student. Russell Dudley, however, was very much involved in politics in high school and afterwards. Although he was greatly affected by his father and the Unity Movement, his view of the world was much more eclectic. Russell Dudley was the head of the Student Representative Council at Livingstone in 1977, his final year at the school. In some ways he became the mediator between students and teachers at Livingstone as well as Livingstone and the other Western Cape black high schools that formed a super Student Representative Council.

Russell Dudley is both thoughtful and reflective, and being the son of a Unity Movement and educational leader has had a great influence on his life. But it is important to again stress that he is neither a political nor pedagogical clone of his father. At a very young age and throughout his high school years, in fact, his father's political prominence and educator status was something of a burden.

> And one of the things that followed me throughout my school career was my father's reputation. Even at primary school. And I think that was one of the difficult parts of school life. But I think in my case I was always somebody else's son, you know. And I thought about it, I can live with that, but it is difficult as a youngster growing up trying to discover yourself. So you're there and everybody knows who you are—you don't know half the people there, and growing up is about trying to make those connections with your peers and also with adults. No. I didn't really talk about it. I was a shy person when I was young. I suspect even if I didn't talk about it, it did show. And sometimes people used to take the mickey out of you—they used to rag you about your dad. I suppose young people are like that. They are very cruel and they know where you are vulnerable and what the issues are. So that is something that I had to cope with quite early on. (Russell Dudley Interview, 2003)

Richard Dudley was aware of this particular burden on his children. When he spoke about Russell being the head of the SRC, he used the word *fatal* in reference to Russell's position. While Russell Dudley did believe in many of the tenets of Unity Movement politics, he was a searcher beginning at a young age. He spoke with great admiration for Tessa Fairbairn, and he praised his father for recognizing thoughtfulness and intelligence and creativity even if the traits existed outside of the realm of Unity Movement politics.

> But I must say this about him: he had an appreciation also for people who were good in their fields, and I think Tessa was one of those persons. Tessa wasn't prepared to just go over . . . but she was willing to be a facilitator, to allow exploration and interaction. And I think that is one of the aspects of my father that I appreciate, because even though he was one of the pillars of the school he had the capacity to engage with people. (Russell Dudley Interview, 2003)

Russell Dudley's exploration included the film societies at a young age; although they were under the auspices of Unity Movement people and discussion leaders sometimes tried to limit discourse, the movies almost always offered different lenses to understand both South Africa and the world. In high school he began seriously reading in German classes and studied Goethe and Grass among other writers.

> I did German at school, and the most interesting thing about German was reading the works of various philosophers in German—existentialism, racialism, and so on. Reading about them and

> discovering that, you know, the way they interpret the world—it wasn't black and white, collaboration, noncollaboration—that was what I used to think about. There was middle ground. (Russell Dudley Interview, 2003)

Faiza Bardien, who was a student at Livingstone in the late 1960s and came back as an English and German teacher, remembers trying to teach Marxist concepts in German class at the same time Russell Dudley was a student. "I could draw on Brecht's poems. I think I'm correct in saying the learners loved the old Kurt Weill compositions—'The Solidarity Song,' 'The Bread of the People,' 'Who is the Party?' " (Bardien Interview, 2003)

Russell Dudley took this sense of exploration into his work as the head of the SRC at Livingstone as well as in his participation in the Western Cape SRC. Interestingly, as he reflects on having political views that transcended the Unity Movement, he remembers expectations and pressures from his parents' comrades; son was supposed to be like father. Although Russell Dudley does not remember verbalizing his distaste for these influences at the time, and even though he respected his father's politics, he clearly acted to broaden both his politics and his view of the world.

> I think because of my experience of how I was being socialised, how my father was always being in advance ahead of me, I couldn't really follow my own shadow; I think I felt a subconscious need to find people who were freer thinking, who wanted to engage with me because of who I was as a person, and that is something that I started discovering at school and outside school. (Russell Dudley Interview, 2003)

The Western Cape SRC was loosely organized and schools formed themselves into geographical cells. For example, there would be a Grassy Park cell, Athlone cell, and so on. Livingstone was part of the Claremont cell. It is fair to say that there were students who affiliated with the Unity Movement, African National Congress, Pan African Congress, and the Black Consciousness Movement amongst the political students at Livingstone. However, the political diversity was even more the case at the cell and provincial levels. While his father recollects Russell being shunned by students in the larger SRC, Russell Dudley was involved. He believed that it was important that each of the different political organizations had a voice. Although he was sympathetic to and stated the concerns of his father and other people in the Unity Movement—political thoughtfulness, the importance of education, police danger and more—he allied with fellow students who believed that it was time for some different type of action against the apartheid regime. Somehow he was able to walk a very fine line between education for (liberation) before education. As his final year in high school came to an end he left the country to further his education in England, and it was after his return, in 1979, that he became more involved with other young people who would become part of the United Democratic Front, the organization that his father and comrades viewed as promoting action for the sake of action in the 1980s.

Politics and Education in the 1980s

As the 1970s were coming to an end, leading to larger student protests in 1980 and even more intense opposition to the growing overt government oppression in 1985, Richard Dudley and his comrades continued to educate their students both politically and academically. In some ways their attempts were futile in terms of keeping young people off the streets and out of risk. The tide had turned. Venues for Dudley's politics had changed even before Soweto, however, as different organizations became the avenue for his political opposition. With organizations like the ANC and PAC banned and individual members of the Unity Movement and Teachers' League of South Africa under personal banning orders, political opposition moved to the neighborhood civic organizations and the growing nonracial sports movement. Dudley and Unity Movement leaders like Dawood Parker, Joe Ebrahim, Polly Slingers, and others helped to revive and expand the fellowships through the civic organizations. Traditionally the neighborhood civics had focused on issues of social welfare and self-help, but people with Unity Movement ideas saw these organizations as a way to reintroduce political education and opposition.

> There was shall I say a ferment at a certain level that was being maintained. And then we were able to get a number of these civic organizations started in different areas and we brought them together under a federation of civic associations in the Western Cape. You must remember that the political organizations were banned at the time. I had to look at things in a somewhat different way, and that is where I landed in doing a lot of political work outside, getting the civic organizations and the fellowships onto their feet again, and getting the civic organizations to do the kind of political tasks that could not be carried out by the political organizations that were banned. I think that they did extremely well and that created this opportunity for us to revive the Unity Movement. We were the teachers and the recruiters because this thing filtered thru to the schools as well, so we could actually pick and choose people who showed a tendency to want to grapple with these things. (Dudley Interview, 2005)

In Dudley's view, the other organization that helped revive the Unity Movement in the early 1980s was the South African Council on Sports (SACOS), whose president was Dudley's comrade, Joe Ebrahim. While Dudley did play soccer and cricket a bit as a teenager, he was not particularly keen on sports as an adult. There is some irony because like some of his other comrades, he viewed sports as a diversion away from the fight for a democratic society. When we had a conversation about sport as an "opiate," however, he spoke very gently on the need for escape as long as escape does not become a way of life. He also asserted the value of the nonracial sports movement because the protests advertised the evils of apartheid throughout the world. There is again some irony, however, because Dudley helped pen slogans like "no normal sport in an abnormal society" that turned up on placards both in South Africa and at world sport events including the United States Open Tennis Championships and the Olympic Games.

The growth of the civic organizations, fellowships, and the nonracial sports movement helped nurture both the rebirth of the New Unity Movement (NUM) and active political meetings during the struggle years. Both NUM and the fellowships were central to Richard Dudley's political life throughout the 1980s. The last year of the 1970s, however, was a tragic year for the Dudley family. Political comrade and friend Ben Kies died, and while that was a great blow to both Unity Movement politics and to the Dudley family personally, the death of Victor Wessels, who was comrade, colleague, and most importantly a trusted, respected, and loved friend, caused even greater pain. Dudley referred to Wessels as an extension of the family. The most tragic event for Iris, Richard, Gary, and Russell Dudley was the death of daughter and older sister Nerine, who was killed in a September automobile accident in the Eastern Cape. While neither Richard nor Iris Dudley spoke very much about Nerine during our conversations, it was Russell Dudley who told me that his sister and father were close, that they talked with each other a lot, and often the conversations blurred the personal and political, much like Richard Dudley's life. Nerine was a medical doctor and at the time of her death was getting a second degree in law. She was working as a doctor in the Eastern Cape, and like Gary Dudley, she was working with people who were oppressed by the apartheid regime. Both Russell and Gary Dudley allude to Nerine's radical politics but there is no definitive proof. Iris Dudley briefly mentioned that she was thinking of going into exile, but again there is no evidence of a plan. What we do know for certain is that the family was devastated by the accident, and Richard Dudley cites her death as one of the factors that led to his retirement from teaching a few years later.

As the 1980s began and both oppression and resistance hardened, teaching and politics for democracy continued. The year 1980 was a particularly intense time in the schools as young activist teachers formed the Teachers' Action Committee (TAC), and students through the Committee of Eighty-One boycotted schooling and protested and marched against both gutter education and more generally the apartheid regime. The student organization was launched in April, and besides Cape Town schools there was representation from rural schools in the Western Cape (Molteno, 1987,

p. 45). TAC was a short-lived group but marked the beginnings of an activist counterpoint to both conservative teachers and socialist Teachers' Leaguers. As Dudley still grieved for Nerine, he tried to keep Livingstone students safe and educate young people through the fellowships and civics. Coloured students boycotted schools, first in February and then again in April, and while the government tried ease things by repairing some school buildings and reducing school fees, they also reacted with more consistent violence to student protests. Besides protesting for resources, students argued that the purpose of gutter education was to train black people to be cheap labor. That was not the case at Livingstone and some other schools, but they were the exception that made the rule. In addition, the Committee of Eighty-One spoke out against police violence, making placards and chanting, "Peaceful students protest, but police riot" (Bickford-Smith, van Heyningen, Worden, 1999, p. 201). More than ever Dudley and his comrades feared for the safety of activist students. While the Committee of Eighty-One first voted to keep protests within school grounds, there was often movement into the streets, and police did not always stop at the school gates. The April 22 Athlone march saw students take to the streets but then back down in the face of police violence near Athlone High School (Molteno, 1987, pp. 52–54). There was tension within Livingstone High School in 1980 as well as subsequent years as some teachers, Faiza Bardien for example, and some students, such as the current Prime Minister of the Western Cape, Ebrahim Rassool, instigated more action. Bardien, whom we briefly met earlier in the chapter, is an interesting case study. Her uncle taught at Livingstone and was a lifelong member of the Unity Movement. Her father was very political and spent time in prison and under house arrest, but he was not affiliated with the Non-European Unity Movement. Bardien was involved in the South Peninsula Educational Fellowship and the New World Film Society, but she took her master's degree in colonial literature; although she held very dearly to her mission as a teacher, she moved her affiliations to the United Democratic Front, Western Cape Teachers Union, and eventually the South African Democratic Teachers Union. As she stressed education she also accompanied students to demonstrations at other schools.

> Because teaching was a mission, I went along with the rest of the staff in breaking the school boycott: we sent learners work sheets so that they could carry on with their learning. And we taught them on Saturdays and in vacations. No wonder we were seen as strike breakers, as bourgeois, opposed to the people's struggles, no wonder other schools often threatened to invade LHS to stage a mass rally on our premises. At the same time I supported the SRC and assisted in their meeting/deliberations with other SRCs in the 1980/1985 boycotts, I certainly did counter the staff's opposition to the learners'

> desire to act and the staff members' derision of "actions uninformed by theoretical understanding." (Bardien Interview, 2003)

In 1980 Dudley was in charge of the school because Evans took ill and went on leave. Dudley and his comrades tried to do two things: (1) continue and even magnify the political lessons on world imperialism and the stages of socialist revolution they had begun teaching even before the Sharpeville Massacre in 1960; (2) provide students with the opportunity to continue their academic studies in the midst of the beginnings of the liberation before education struggle years.

> We were trying to give these protests political meaning because these pupils were out there marching, saying that they wanted equality in the schools, and they would continue to boycott until their demands were met, and so on. And, of course, the police were beating the daylights out of them. But we wanted them to give these protests a political content and direction, so we taught these people to think in the way of the priorities. The things that you're asking for are the things that come to citizens in this country, so you must, therefore, demand your basic rights as citizens—your franchise. You must have your vote. We didn't want these pupils to lose the momentum of their studies, so we used to provide them with the study guides that they could utilize at school and home, and we worked together with the parents and the pupils. We used to print their assignment for them and get them to do this sort of thing and deliver it the following day because we pointed out to them that they can't be on the street all the time. They've got to be at home sometime, and they've got to spend that time properly. The call went out to the pupils that they must take control of their schools, and it took a terrible turn, and this was particularly so in Mitchells Plain and these other areas, because they said to hell with the education, this was liberation before education. (Dudley Interview, 1999)

Education for liberation was not an easy task, however, as student boycotts and activism grew. The *Inter-School Manual*, a student journal, published an article titled "Teachers—The Stillborn Radicals." The article disparagingly stated, "Our first, our second, our final impression of teachers in general, is that they are a misfit lot condemned to the Sewage Tanks of Athlone. Their sole concerns are their checks, their bonds on houses, their cars, and a host of other interests. As a body, they could not be trusted" (Kihn, 2002, p. 84). Students, teachers, and parents took to the streets to demonstrate against gutter education in March, and three teachers from Crystal Senior Secondary School in Hanover Park were fired for instigating the protests. Students at more than thirty schools boycotted classes in April, and as already noted, black schools from throughout the province joined the fight.

The difficulty of keeping students connected to their schoolwork would become more and more problematic throughout the 1980s. South African historian Colin Bundy offers an account of why Dudley and his comrades faced such a difficult task. His analysis combines age and class, and although there are flaws in the argument, he does present a partial explanation for a very complex issue. Bundy argues first that there is something called a "generational consciousness" and second that it existed in South Africa because black youth were closed out of the economic, political, and social system. Both Bundy and William Nasson quote 1980 census statistics that show extremely high unemployment amongst coloured people in Cape Town, and both argue that coloured youth saw no hope living under the apartheid system. If we extend their thinking, we must ask what possible purpose could education serve black youth? Dudley was both angered and saddened because he believed that education was the revolutionary trump card.

Bundy's theory of generational consciousness was also in play amidst the teaching profession. Dudley was upset by young activist teachers, especially some who first taught at Livingstone and then belittled the school because in their view Dudley and his Unity Movement and Teachers' League of South Africa comrades were not aiding students in their fight against a "fascist regime." Richard Rive's books *Emergency* and *Emergency Continued* present a brilliant fictional account of the complexities of the divide with portrayals of Trotskyist, "independent," and activist teachers. More recently Mark Constas uses the lives of two African teachers during the struggle years to equate generation and politics. It is important, however, to remember that "generational consciousness" is at best a small part of the education for (liberation) before education divide. In my oral histories of both Teachers' League of South Africa and Western Cape Teachers Union teachers in *Voices from Cape Town Classrooms*, generation only partially explains the complexities. Dudley and his comrades had foundational beliefs, but they discussed and discussed and struggled with their position. Earlier in the chapter we met Kevin Wildschut, who during the struggle years was a younger activist teacher. Wildschut reflected on the difficult decisions teachers made at the time:

> It was a very difficult time because we all hold education very dear. I think there's no teacher who will say education is not important. What we were doing, our process was some of the slogans of the day like "liberation before education." And we were saying we're teaching liberation education. So it was a mixture of classroom academic work as well as teaching and informing learners about the need to radicalize, to change what was happening in our country, and to be part of the process of change. So when learners came to me and said

> to me, "Sir, should I study for my exams?" my response would always be twofold. "Yes, you should because it's going to be necessary in the future. But at the same time you cannot neglect to study the real history of today, the history that you're learning today." (Wildschut Interview, 1999)

Student activism with the support of progressive teachers, as well as the beginning of links between students and workers, grew in the early years of the 1980s. Teachers who came of age in the 1970s and 1980s, in spite of being mentored and sometimes parented by Teachers' Leaguers, joined together under the auspices of the Congress Movement, more specifically under the banner of the United Democratic Front that was founded in 1983. While Dudley and his comrades were preparing to launch (or re-launch) the New Unity Movement, the ANC and PAC, as well as other black consciousness organizations, were reinvigorated in the wake of the 1980 demonstrations. William Nasson describes the different groups that took hold in the Western Cape between 1980 and 1985. Although NUM, the other new Unity Movement organization of the time, the Cape Action League (CAL), the ANC, and PAC did unite on certain actions, the alliances were always short-lived and the longstanding disagreements quickly returned. NUM critiqued the ANC for its capitalist ideology and makes the argument even more forcefully at the present time, while the ANC viewed NUM as sitting in the grandstands. Dudley was especially affected by the ANC rebirth at the time, and the issue was personal. Although he still made the same noncollaborationist, nonracialist, and anti-imperialist arguments, he was especially concerned because Livingstone students were influenced by the UDF and even worse by the lure of UMKHONTO WE SIZWE. Dudley speaks specifically of Patrick Marks and Geraldine Fraser-Moleketi, who were both exceptional students at Livingstone and who took different paths in the armed resistance. Marks was killed while in exile, and Dudley is convinced that his death was due to his disagreement with MK policy. Fraser-Moleketi is currently the minister of Welfare and Population Development.

> I didn't know that they were going. They would leave school surreptitiously. Now, this is another little sort of thing, my reading of the situation. I think that when those events occurred in 1976 and again when things began to boil up in 1985, then the ANC from outside was prodding this sort of thing, using quite a lot of literature that they posted into South Africa and also spread amongst the students because this was the major way in which they recruited young people in very large numbers into the ranks of UMKHONTO WE SIZWE. The students were being hammered by the police and the army, and they left the country in droves. Well, the fact of the matter is that certain of them came to find ways and means out of

> South Africa because they told me that they wanted to come join the armed forces outside. I told them that if you leave from here an ignoramus, that's the worst that could happen to you. Now, they are celebrating the death of these martyrs, and so on, but they didn't have a dog's chance of doing anything other than blowing themselves up. (Dudley Interview, 2003)

The United Democratic Front (UDF) was launched in Mitchell's Plain in 1983; through a leadership of clergy, teachers, and women's and civic organizations, the UDF became the voice of activist protest in the Western Cape until members were banned and arrested, and the organization was banned following the more intense 1985 student boycotts. At the launch, the Reverend Allan Boesak, one of Dudley's least favorite people, declared: "We want all our rights, we want them here and we want them now." Boesak's words, of course, exemplify both the action for the sake of action and the radical naivety that Dudley and other members of the Unity Movement so abhorred.

At the same time that the UDF came into being, Dudley and his comrades took a more public presence in both NUM and the TLSA. The decision to launch NUM was made by Dudley, other Teachers' Leaguers, members of the South Peninsula Educational Fellowship (SPEF) and other Civics and Fellowships, and the South African Council On Sport at Joe Ebrahim's house in Elfindale. Comrades in the Eastern Cape, Transkei, Ciskei, and Natal were contacted, and numbers grew as members of the Unity Movement began to come back into South Africa from exile. Dudley reflected on the organization's view at the time:

> The revolution does not rise upon people's anger alone. If you are going to overthrow the existing order and establish another in its place, you must not only have the ideas that give you an understanding of your position as it is now, but you must be able to use your insight into the development of political struggles to give you an idea of what you are going to be coming up against. (Dudley Interview, 2003)

At the same time, the Teachers' League commenced reissuing some of their classic publications that made similar arguments: the work of people such as Ben Kies, Edgar Maurice, Willem van Schoor, Hosea Jaffee, and the infamous black consciousness articles. William Nasson points out that republication of this literature "serves to highlight the close association in the Unity Movement between historical production and the national liberation struggle" (Nasson, 1990, p. 199). In addition, Christopher Saunders speaks to the intellectual depth of the publications in his historiography text, *The Making of the South African Past: Major Historians on Race and Class*. It was not always easy finding originals because when the apartheid government began banning political teachers in the 1950s, many people stashed away any literature that might be deemed "communistic" by the state. Numerous Unity Movement people and some of their children told me about not being able to find or recover hidden documents. Anthony Hess, who is a school principal in Grabow, a rural town thirty miles east of Cape Town in the grape and apple growing country, was an active member of both WECTU and the ANC. He laughed about digging up the garden in the 1990s at the bequest of his father, who was also a school principal and a strident Teachers' Leaguer, in order to find books and articles that were buried in previous decades. Nothing was found. Dudley's hidden papers met a similar fate.

> I had hidden a number of documents of the Teachers' League and the Unity Movement, and this is the sad thing about it. I had hidden this at the home of one of the relatives and this chap got a fright. Without telling me he had dug a hell of a big hole and dumped the stuff. I learned about it when I went to check up, and they were completely ruined. The second thing is that there was an underground chamber in the neighbourhood that I thought would be a useful place as well. What I didn't reckon with was that this chamber was very much lower than sea level and it filled with water. I'm absolutely mad at myself when I think back on the valuable material that went wasted. (Dudley Interview, 2005)

The New Unity Movement, the Struggle, and the End of Apartheid

When Dudley became the President of the New Unity Movement, he was still grieving for Nerine and also trying to recover from a rather serious reoccurrence of the heart problems that first appeared a decade earlier. In 1984 he decided that it was time to end his career as a teacher. His political work, although it sounds absurd, was becoming more extensive, and he felt that he could not devote full energy to both politics and the school. Since Gary and Russell had completed their university years, family expenses had lightened, and although Dudley refers to his state retirement as a scurvy pension, he had begun saving money ten years earlier because he was fearful of both detention and his heart condition. Retirement from Livingstone, of course, did not mean disengagement, although Richard and Iris Dudley did embark on a trip to England in 1985, the most intense of the struggle years. Richard Dudley's life became even more interesting upon his and Iris's return from their journey.

Student protests in 1985 are described in depth in *Emergency Continued*. Through Alex Dreyer's life, Richard Rive jumps twenty-five years in the history of apartheid to portray the complexities of oppression and resistance. Dreyer describes a day in the life of school in a letter to his old comrade, Abraham Hanslo, who lives in exile in Canada and whose character is very much Unity Movement in *Emergency*:

> A typical day will start quite normally with the expectation of lessons. Then the pupils decide to have a mass anti-apartheid rally at the school or at some other venue. The end of any teaching for that day. Posters, chanting, slogans, toyi-toyiing and speakers exhorting the crowd to action, any action. On any one such day we might have up to four thousand pupils in our grounds drawn from all over the Peninsula. Then the police arrive in Casspirs and armoured trucks and give the crowd a few minutes in which to disperse. They usually ignore the order. Then follows either a baton charge, the police flaying with quirts and sjamboks, or the shooting of tear-gas canisters. The pupils retaliate with stones and any missiles they can find. We stand by angry and impotent, trying to reason with whoever is prepared to speak to us. By midday I have had enough and get into my car and drive home. Once in Elfindale (where Dudley lives) people are walking their dogs, washing their cars or shopping in the main road. They are not unconcerned about the happenings but are ten million miles away from the action which they read about in their newspapers or see on their television screens. (Rive, 1990, p. 4)

Rive breathes life into important events like student protests and placard demonstrations, the proposed UDF march to Pollsmoor Prison to demand the release of Nelson Mandela, school boycotts, the Trojan Horse incident, the provincial head of Coloured Education, Carter Ebrahim, closing coloured schools in Cape Town on September 6, and students, teachers, and parents retaking their schools September 17; he uses Alexander Sinton High School in Athlone to portray the last item on the list. It is a story that Vivienne Carelse also tells in *Voices*, and, in fact, the cover of that book has a picture from the school on September 17 with students sitting on the Sinton wall holding placards. One sign read, "We do not want violence. We want our schools—they belong to us." Dudley was in the crowd at Sinton that day, he recalls Dullah Omar's wife standing with a handbag in one hand and a rock in the other. More importantly he remembers police shooting rubber bullets into the crowd. He escaped into the car of a NUM comrade. Carelse provides a more detailed description from inside of the school:

> In fact, in eighty-five we had the re-opening of schools on September 17. We had a re-opening where the community, parents, teachers, and students re-opened. We reclaimed our school because it had

> been closed by the education minister. We went there in the morning, we were going to unlock the school, the principal and the staff. We were going to enter and occupy the school, and try to have a normal day. The minute we got onto the premises the police came. They used to park on this field opposite our school. These huge yellow trucks, those huge Casspirs. They kept them there almost permanently during that period, and they just came onto the premises and started loading up. They arrested people. They filled about four of those normal standard police vans with parents and teachers. And they sat there baking in the sun because the community, the parents outside, decided they were going to barricade the school. They parked in the road on the pavements all around. Our school is on a corner on a suburban block. And on all the surrounding roads they had blocked it off so that no additional police vans could get onto the premises or get off. So there was a state of siege for a good few hours at that school until they mowed down a fence and drove through to take the people away. We were all arrested that day. About 197 of us were arrested for opening our school. We were held in Mannenberg Police Station for the whole day until the lawyers negotiated our release. (Carelse Interview, 1999)

The government arrested people viewed as opposition throughout the 1980s but the numbers intensified in 1985. Many of the people arrested were teachers, and the UDF was especially targeted during and after the 1985 events. Police would make sweeps arresting many people on the same day and time. Helen Kies, the editor of the *Educational Journal*, was detained for a month after demonstrations at Harold Cressy High School where she taught. She laughed after the fact because she was one of the teachers who, following the education for liberation tenets of the Teachers' League, did not support the school boycotts. Dudley expected to be arrested, and his time came late in 1985. Gary Dudley was teaching and living at home at the time, and he remembers the police coming in the early morning dark and yelling for his father as they knocked hard on the door. Gary's room was at the front of the house, and he peeked out of the door and then went to tell his father who, of course, was already awakened by the commotion. Richard Dudley remembers the event with great detail, and it should be no surprise at this point in the story that he used his detention as a teachable moment. First, he describes his arrest:

> Then they came. I was one of many. They came to my home around about four o'clock, five o'clock in the morning. My son Gary was here, but at the time I think Russell was on his own. It was 1985. Gary and Russell had been looking after the place when Iris and I were overseas. In any event they told me that they wanted to see

> my study. They said to me that they want to search the place. I pointed out that I hadn't even had breakfast and they said that you can go and have breakfast. One of their men watched me, so I had breakfast that morning under the watchful eye of the security police. I told Gary to watch whatever they took and that they must give us a receipt. This chap who was in charge looked at the books on the shelves and said in Afrikaans, "I don't understand all these things, I'm not going to go through all these things." So they just picked up some Journals and one or two other things as well, which they returned to me incidentally. That would have been just one year after I left teaching. They took me away. There were four of them. Two of them sat on either side of me on the back seat. These individuals were very aggressive, I would say. They're big fellows. I'm not very small, but they wanted to make me feel very small. Gary had stayed with my wife so she could get over that. They allowed me to take my pajamas and toothpaste, and soap, etc. . . I just said goodbye to her and off I went with them. (Dudley Interview, 2003)

The teachable moment, of course, came during the interrogation.

> Then they took me to the offices at Caledon Square, and they handed me over to the interrogation officers. They wanted to know why people are behaving the way in which they were. I said to them that I don't know the people who are organizing these things because I'd been overseas. I'd just come back. He said why do these children go and break things at the schools like the windows. At that time the amount of destruction was terrible. They break the buses, etc. . . . So I said to them I've never asked them about this but what I do know is the population is angry. I said my own organization doesn't work that way, but this is happening. I said there is absolutely nothing that I can do to help you stop this. I proceeded to tell them about this anger that people had by comparing the position of the people in Bishopscourt to the people in the Cape Flats. I drew the parallel in this manner. I said the people up in Bishopscourt have all the stones in the world available around them but they don't throw stones. The people on the Cape Flats live in sandy waste. They don't have stones there, but they're so angry that they look for stones and bricks to throw. So now one must ask oneself why they are doing this. I said, well, I know that a lot of people up there in Bishopscourt are pretty wealthy people, they have good jobs. They are able to live in peace and quiet there. And they're able to send their children to school and to provide them with all of the necessary things. At home the children are

> assured of having the proper food and also a place to study, all the conveniences. Then they can choose to study the things that are going to lead up to many occupations that are open to them. They've got a protected life that they are very positive about. If you go down to the Cape Flats most of the people are out of work. Secondly, they're not sure of their jobs, and then the conditions in the schools are bad. The places are bedeviled by violence and so on. There is no security there. The parents are not all violent, but the children are very angry and they're concerned about this. They have become very angry because of the way in which the children have been treated. I said that over all these years these things have been happening—the people just cannot take it anymore. And this is the way in which they burst out as they do. I said that I know from my point of view they think they can get all these things right by staying away from school. They are not doing their examinations; that's not the way which we see it. We would prefer them to be in school, but we can't make them get back into school. Because you have made it impossible for them to want to go back to school. (Dudley Interview, 2003)

Because of his heart problems Dudley was released from custody following his interrogation. He had a letter about an appointment with his cardiologist, Tom Mabin, that was scheduled for the following day, and it is his conclusion that because of the worldwide fury over Steve Biko's death in detainment, the South African government was very careful regarding health with people they imprisoned. Of course, it did not stop the government from assassinating opponents of apartheid at the time. Dudley escalated his political activity through NUM after his arrest, and he kept abreast of events at Livingstone. He was also asked by teachers at other schools to address students—this was through his TLSA work—and requests came from Livingstone students who were teaching throughout the Cape Flats in the 1980s. He recalled speaking with students in Belhar, a group areas suburb on the north side of Cape Town adjacent to the University of the Western Cape.

> I drew your attention to the case of Es'kia Mphahlele, that in 1952 when he sought the help of the ANC, Mandela had actually told him that the reconstruction should wait upon the revolution. And Mandela's been very quiet on that sort of thing, because when they came up with the slogan, "Liberation before Education," it was actually to negate what we had been trying to drum into people's heads, that the struggle in education was, in fact, part and parcel of the struggle for liberation, and you couldn't halt it and then start it up again. It was a continuous thing because you cannot create a

> revolution with ignorant people. You can have a revolt. You can have a rebellion, but you cannot have a revolution without education. I once went out to Belhar in the 1980s to go and speak there to pupils, and I explained to pupils who were present there, for example, when they said that they were going to boycott school until the government met all their demands, then what you're saying is that in this way you can then gain demands which the government has been denying people on very powerful political and economic grounds simply by staying out of school. I said that I know how you feel, but you must understand the nature of struggle inside and outside the school, otherwise you would simply be chasing shadows. (Dudley Interview, 2005)

So while the second half of the 1980s saw more bannings, arrests, and extreme apartheid violence, there were also secret talks between the government, corporate leaders, and the African National Congress. Andre Brink's 1986 open letter to President Botha exposes apartheid horror and both the anguish and anger of those who fought the apartheid regime. After condemning Botha for the murder and destruction in Crossroads, a Cape Town township where more than 500,000 people were left homeless after government violence, Brink portrays the lies Botha and apartheid lived.

> You try to convince gullible Western leaders like Reagan and Thatcher that you are in fact a Great Reformer. So you scrap the Mixed Marriages Act, but then forbid married people from different races to live together where they choose. You end the forced removal of whole communities; then unfortunate incidents like Crossroads happen to "encourage" the homeless to move voluntarily. You abolish the pass laws, then set about arresting countless blacks for "trespassing" in white-owned areas. You bring a handful of coloured and Indian people into parliament and offer them an illusion of power-sharing, but the moment they hesitate to collaborate in passing some of the most draconian legislation this country has ever seen, you treat them like schoolboys—and then press on with the legislation regardless. You announce that you will discuss constitutional reform with black leaders, while ensuring that the true leaders of the people are kept in jail or detention. You assure the world that this is a free country, yet since long before the State of Emergency the meekest peaceful protests have been brutally broken up. You tell us you are a Christian, yet you send in your forces to fire tear-gas at funeral processions, forcing the mourners to drop their coffins in the road. And when we profess we cannot believe you, you try to end all criticism by imposing the Big Silence. (Brink, 1998, pp. 22, 23)

In spite of Botha and escalating state violence against apartheid opposition, the minister of justice initially met with Mandela in 1985. There were also unofficial talks in Tanzania, Senegal, Burkina Faso, Ghana, Zimbabwe, and London, and by 1988, with worldwide anti-apartheid pressure mounting, the African independence movement flourishing, and military losses in Angola, the talks had become very serious. NUM made approaches to both the ANC and PAC, and both organizations, as well as the South African Communist Party (SACP), sent feelers to NUM, but the differences between the groups that were exhibited in the 1950s were still present. Dudley himself was in contact with Walter Sisulu in Johannesburg, and other NUM comrades had discussions with Govan Mbeki in the Eastern Cape. Contact was also made with Mandela, but the divide was too wide. NUM did work with organized labor, however, and the organization was invited to a major political conference sponsored by the Congress of South African Trade Unions (COSATU). The New Unity Movement turned down the invitation. (NUM, 1988)

Beginning in 1988, partially because Dudley was the president of NUM and partially because he believed in dialogue, the ANC and SACP began making personal approaches concerning democratic unity; the meetings continued through the 1990s. Sidney Mufamadi, who was a member of the SACP and became the minister of security in Mandela's government, and Graeme Bloch, who was a UDF leader, came on different missions that first year. When I asked Dudley why these people were sent to him, the answer was direct. "They were sent along to talk to me because I would have been prepared to talk to them, to discuss it. If they had gone to any of the other officials, they would have told them to go to hell" (Dudley Interview, 2005). Mufamadi came to seek Dudley's aid in affiliating NUM with the COSATU conference. Mufamadi and Dudley spoke in Dudley's dining room, and Mufamadi argued that NUM's socialist voice was important in the fight against liberalism and capitalism, a foreshadowing of what was to come in postapartheid South Africa. Dudley made it clear to Sidney Mufamadi that NUM could not betray the organization's stands on nonracialism and noncollaboration. The emissaries would continue through the 1994 democratic election. Partially because of the choices exhibited by Dudley above, however, NUM both was not and chose not to be a player in the transition from apartheid to Mandela, nor in the postapartheid South African government.

The process of ending apartheid moved quickly between 1989 and 1994. Although violence and oppression continued right up to the election, it was clear that one way or another, in relative peace or ultimate civil war, apartheid would end. Besides the continuing not-so-secret negotiations, events in Africa and the world called on President de Klerk to end apartheid. When the Berlin Wall came down in November 1989 as the Soviet Union died, both Margaret Thatcher and the first President Bush magnified their pressure on de Klerk. Although Thatcher had called the ANC thugs and terrorists, she publicly warned de Klerk to stop interfering with the new South-West

African People's Organisation's (SWAPO) independent government of Namibia. In addition, some of her subordinates began meeting with anti-apartheid opposition, including representatives of the African National Congress. Bush, for his part, invited Albertina Sisulu, the feminist leader and wife of ANC stalwart Walter Sisulu, to represent the ANC in talks with United States government officials. The West threatened South Africa economically through both divestment and World Bank/International Monetary Fund loan recalls. Thus, on February 2, 1990, de Klerk spoke before the legislature announcing that political prisoners would be freed immediately and that opposition organizations and individuals would be unbanned. Nine days later, at 4:00 p.m., as the world watched via television, the seventy-one-year-old Nelson Mandela walked out of prison after spending over 10,000 days as a political prisoner. Interestingly, in over 200 hours of interviews with Richard Dudley, he has never mentioned that day. In contrast, other progressive teachers in South Africa can describe the moment in detail—not only the release but where they were, what they were doing, what they were thinking, and the magnitude of the event. One of those teachers, Jeff Cohen, taught during the struggle years under the mentorship of Yusuf da Costa and then in Langa before becoming a teacher and finally principal at Herzlia High School, the Jewish day school in Cape Town:

> There I was sitting in Langa on second February with all my colleagues. It was a nonracial staff, and there's de Klerk saying the ban on the ANC is lifted with immediate effect. And we all just leapt and cheered. And he said that Mandela's going to be released and I can't describe the feeling. I can picture it. I can live it. I can smell it. The atmosphere, the summer day, the dust in the air. And driving home that day, I just remember I had the windows of my car open and I put my hand out the window because I felt the air must feel different! It's like the world has changed. Mandela's coming out. The ANC is legal. What's happened here is a miracle, a miracle. (Cohen Interview, 1999)

The release of Mandela was followed in 1991 by the abolition of the Group Areas Act and a plan for token school integration of formerly white schools. NUM analysis of the situation, as well as that of Dudley, held to noncollaboration because they believed that the relaxing of apartheid was merely a means of the former apartheid state including the black bourgeoisie, or the black bourgeoisie-to-be in the form of the ANC, in worldwide capitalist imperialism. NUM published numerous critiques of the talks and accused the African National Congress of collaborating with the Nationalist Party to enter the capitalist Western world. However, members of the organization did participate in discussions and public panels with people from the ANC as well as PAC and the SACP in order to bring their socialist critique as well as their views on nonracialism and noncollaboration to public arenas. Dudley spoke with me about two such occasions before the 1994 election. One was a forum where he shared the platform with Dullah Omar, his one-time Unity Movement comrade who moved to the UDF and ANC during the mid-1980s and became the Minister of Justice in the first democratic government in 1994. While Dudley could be very critical of Omar, he also spoke with fondness and respect. In his long essay on struggle politics in the Western Cape in *All, Here, and Now: Black Politics in South Africa in the 1980s*, William Nasson argues that Dullah Omar's Unity Movement roots of nonracialism and anti-imperialism were ever-present in his ANC politics. Dudley did not think so the night he shared the podium at the University of Cape Town. Omar presented the coming of a new South Africa and the hope and possibilities for democracy. Dudley, on the other hand, argued that it was not the socialist revolution that would bring the equality necessary for democracy. While the evening was civil, the divide was clear.

The second event that Dudley participated in also preceded the 1994 election. Like every personal or organizational invitation, NUM decided collectively whether or not to participate. This was also true, however, in the workings of the ANC, PAC, and the SACP. The Black Lawyers Association held a forum in Johannesburg; Dudley represented NUM, Barney Desai PAC, and Mandela spoke for the ANC. The proceedings were hosted by Ndumisa Ntsebeza, who later chaired the Amnesty Committee of the Truth and Reconciliation Commission. Dudley recalls that Mandela was very late and that both he and Desai had made their presentations by the time Mandela arrived. Dudley's comments reflected on the position of the Unity Movement historically as well as at the time. Mandela argued that the ANC was the only South African liberation force, and he was extremely critical of PAC. Dudley also recalls that many people in the audience were unhappy with Mandela's intensity, but in the end the three participants embraced as the meeting concluded.

There were many bumps throughout 1993 with breaks in negotiations and real possibilities of civil war. The most worrisome time was in April when Chris Hani, the brilliant young Communist leader whom Andre Brink refers to as "the soldier with Shakespeare," was assassinated. While the murder of this man, who represented the hope of the new South Africa, was tragic enough, the arrogant and oppressive subsequent behavior of the "peacemaker," President de Klerk, fueled the flames of violence and civil war. Brink's essay, "The Dove in the Grave," tells the story of Hani's funeral with metaphoric horror but then possibilities. When the coffin was put in the ground, a group of white doves, the symbol of peace, were set free, but one of them fell right into the grave. After a number of speeches, including one in which Nelson Mandela called for reconciliation while ANC and SACP youth booed, a young comrade jumped into the grave and again set the dove free—the coming of the new South Africa?

With all the hiccups, Nelson Mandela became president of South Africa on May 10, 1994. The world watched as he took the oath of office, and apartheid was dead. Of course, as we have already stated numerous times, the new South Africa was not the democracy of Dudley and his comrades. Their strong belief that capitalist imperialism still ruled South Africa necessitated their continuing stance of noncollaboration. One of the most emboldened examples of such is that Dudley and many of his comrades boycotted the 1994 elections. Reflecting on Reflections: Conclusions and Considerations of the Present, the final chapter of the book, analyzes the life of Richard Dudley through the tenets that have shaped his teaching and politics and are all part of his fight for a democratic South Africa.

8

reflecting on reflections

Conclusions and Considerations of the Present

At the Dudley home in Elfindale there are three rooms that are used as libraries, although there are books in every room of the house. Above Richard Dudley's workspace sit census tract records with information on class, race, gender, education, work, and more. Among the books sitting out on various desks and tables are works of Chomsky, Gramsci, and recent critiques of capitalism and development in southern Africa. On the shelves with *Das Kapital* are science books, Penguin paperbacks, medical books for granddaughter Meegan, C. P. Snow, Peter Abrahams, Robert Owen, Richard Rive, Hogben's *Mathematics for the Million*, E. H. Carr, Tolstoy, Shakespeare, Huxley, Hesse, an autobiography of Tony Leon, *Long Walk to Freedom*, Tolkien, Elizabeth Allende, Orwell, South African history, Bessie Head, and much, much more. Dudley reminds me that many of his books have been "borrowed" but will not return. Scattered throughout the rooms are photographs from Livingstone, various posters, an award certificate from the Islamic Unity Convention—Dudley is an atheist—and a 1990 New Unity Movement Youth Wing calendar that visually helps explain how anti-imperialism, nonracialism, and nocollaboration continue in Richard Dudley's life at the present time. Pictured on the calendar are Mao, Marx, and Lenin with Tabata and Dora Taylor. 1990 was the year that Nelson Mandela was released from prison and talks between the Nationalist Party and the ANC were in full swing without any influence from Mao, Marx, Lenin, Tabata, Taylor, or for that matter, Richard Dudley. For Dudley, however, not being involved was an ideological decision that relates back to his life as teacher and comrade that we have witnessed in the preceding chapters.

> To suggest that we simply accept the dictates of overseas sponsors and negotiate with the ruling class and its allies is unacceptable. To suggest further that negotiation is 'inevitable' is no better than saying that death is inevitable. We are at one with Zeph Mothopeng when he says, categorically, that negotiation is out of the question. . . . We are convinced, on the basis of our political understanding of struggles here, and on the basis of outcomes of 'negotiated settlements' in the neo-colonial world, that all the present talk of 'negotiations' is a cruel hoax. It is a hoax offered to embattled millions reeling under a violent and oppressive society that cannot be patched up; whether by talks, talks about talks, racist reforms or by the weight of slush funds with which nation-wide efforts to head off truly democratic change are being pursued. It must be overturned and re-built upon the foundations of universal democratic principles. (Dudley, 1989, NP)

The Unity Movement and by association Richard Dudley were criticized for four decades for their unbending adherence to the tenets of the Ten Point Programme and their total refusal toward cooperation with the government and more importantly other opposition groups. Furthermore, the organization's socialist anti-imperialism meant that their foundational belief in noncollaboration did not end with the death of apartheid. As we reported in Chapter Seven as well as in the above quotation, Dudley and his comrades did not support the discussions that began in 1985 between the ANC, Nationalist Party, Anglo-American Corporation, and selected representatives of the West. Within the boundaries of NUM's anti-imperialist world view, the only possible outcome of such talks was a capitalist country that adhered to the edicts of imperialism through the dictates of the World Bank and the International Monetary Fund. When the 1994 elections came and almost twenty million people voted, many standing in endless lines in the rain and shedding raindrop-like tears of joy for the end of apartheid and the victory of democracy, Dudley and many of his comrades chose to stay home. In fact, NUM published a banner declaring by suggestion that the ANC had ignored working people in their rush to capitalist collaboration with de Klerk, the IMF, and the World Bank. A direct reference to the vote was included in the document: "Voting will bring none of the things the people have so long struggled, even died, for. So why bother to vote?" (New Unity Movement Flyer, 1994)

Although Hein Marais is not a member of NUM, his book, *South Africa: Limits to Change*, portrays an historical and theoretical rationale for the Unity Movement's lack of participation in the postapartheid government of South Africa. In his 1994 May Day speech, Nelson Mandela assured the nation that South African economic policy did not include nationalization nor was there any connection to Marxism (Marais, 2001, p. 122). The speech contradicted earlier economic statements but according to Marais was true to a process that began before the ANC came to power. In addition, he quietly suggests that the African National Congress historically did not represent or fight for a classless society. As part of the negotiations for South African transition, the ANC was very strong on the political and very weak on the economic. Thus the Bill of Rights and the subsequent Constitution are progressive, and you may not be discriminated against because of "race, gender, sex, pregnancy, marital status, ethnic or social origin, colour, sexual orientation, age, disability, religion, conscience, belief, culture, language or birth" (Marais, 2001, p. 91). There is no mention of class. On the other hand, the economic reality in the new South Africa, a marriage of the ANC, South African and global corporations, and the World Bank and International Monetary Fund, is more neoliberal than it is socialist—in fact it is not socialist at all. Marais documents the ANC journey towards conservative or, if you like, neoliberal economic policy, and he is quick to point out that the ANC was not duped, but rather was a player in the process. Although redistribution policy was part of the conversation and even part of original policy, it at best became subservient in the form of public works and possibly trickle-down theory. In addition, redistribution was harshly criticized by corporate spokesmen and by the International Monetary Fund. Since the ANC's issue was not economics, the organization was "educated" by corporate reports submitted by Nedcor, Old Mutual, and SANLAM (Marais, 2001, p. 127). While there is no debate regarding the new South Africa being less oppressive and more free than apartheid South Africa, and there is no question that racism is less of an issue, it might be that the ANC government has a bit of amnesia when it comes to the blatant reality of class disparity at the present time. Marais does give credit for public works accomplishments, such as electricity, water, housing, pregnancy care, and school nutrition programs. But he suggests that the African National Congress is too proud and chooses not to acknowledge that many of the improvements cannot be afforded by the masses. Finally, there are harsh realities that the government does not address head-on, including unequal education, healthcare, and of course the AIDS pandemic; all are related to the huge economic disparity that remains in the new South Africa. While Hein Marais does not believe that the current reality was or is inevitable, neither is he optimistic:

> The development path embarked upon is already yielding what historian Colin Bundy has called "a lop-sided structure—two nations disguised as one, a hybrid social formation consisting of increasingly deracialised insiders and persistently black outsiders" (1999: p. 11). It is an outcome that bears scant resemblance to the visions of many millions who prosecuted the long struggle against apartheid. But it also hardly jars with an outcome many others—arrayed on either side of yesterday's barricades—quietly wished for. (Marais, 2001, p. 306)

In spite of Marais's analysis, it is not surprising that NUM and Richard Dudley are criticized for not coming to play. Livingstone High School graduates who respect and admire Dudley speak with disappointment. Some, like Sean Goldschmidt, who revered his teachers, are saddened by the boycott of the 1994 election.

> I still have a lot of respect for Dudley, and still think he is extremely intelligent and well read, but politically I have moved on. I feel that his movement is not in touch with what is happening in the country and the world. At one stage they advocate a boycott, now there was no way I was going to support that. I thought here is my chance to vote and make a difference, and although I don't see the ANC as the perfect party, I have a lot of doubt, but I feel it's the best option available politically. (Goldschmidt Interview, 2003)

Ralph Freese speaks in a more pointed way. While respectful of Richard Dudley as a teacher and person, he bemoans not having Dudley as a national leader:

> I am saddened by Dudley because he's clinging to the Unity movement in a way that is a massive loss to the country. I'm not saying that working in the ANC, which I did, was any better, but I think he could have had a much greater influence than he has had. He would have taken an intellectual part into those debates that would have beat the pants off people. He is intellectually way above them. (Freese Interview, 2003)

Richard Dudley knows the criticisms, but he is much more assertive than Marais in his economic/political critique of the ANC and the "democratic" South African government. In 1991 he referred to the negotiations as "betrayal and pantomime" and as a means to end the liberation movement in order to continue the divide between rich and poor (Num, 1991, pp. 3, 4). A year later, in presenting the Jonas Fred Bosch Memorial Lecture, Dudley criticized the ANC for its attempt to join the power elite and accused the World Bank/International Monetary Fund of supporting the rich and hurting the poor.

> This is the very bank that imposed GST on the poor, and now has imposed VAT upon the poor making them poorer. A Bank that has ordered the government to cut out free medical services, to minimize free education, to retrench teachers, to end food subsidies and, at the same time, to grant bigger tax advantages to the business world so that the profits of the capitalist classes should not be threatened. (Num, 1992, p. 18)

Finally, in his 1998 NUM presidential address he again accuses the ANC of abandoning working and poor people as well as denying universal, free, public education; the new South Africa is not viewed by Dudley as a democratic society. Near the end of the speech he outlines the continuing mission of the New Unity Movement and the liberation struggle—this was four years into the new South Africa:

> We say a people united will never be defeated. Let us look beyond all the pomp, all the ceremony, all the hype built around the pop heroes paraded through the country, beyond old and new promises that a captive government will not be allowed to fulfill. Look again at hospitals, schools and decaying city centres; at friends and neighbours cowering in homes, though they may be securely locked, because crime is everywhere. Let us look beyond make believe elections and the pantomime that was the 1994 roadshow. Our duty is to build within our communities and across the nation a powerful united force that can usher in a society that will make every child's heart happy and give every adult the chance to stand tall among his or her equals in a land of peace and plenty. (Num, 1998, p. 24)

In *South Africa: Limits to Change* Marais analyzes the African National Congress, Congress of South African Trade Unions, and South African Communist Party alliance and quotes Ellen Meiksin Wood: "it is not only that we do not know how to *act* against capitalism but that we are forgetting how to think against it" (Marais, 2001, p. 4). Richard Dudley not only thinks and speaks against capitalism, but anti-imperialism remains ever present in his actions. In addition, probably because he cannot help himself, within his actions he is always teaching. Besides his spoken and written words, he continues to live his beliefs and his critique. Two events illustrate both noncollaboration and teaching for democracy: (1) Dudley's reaction to being approached by the ANC in 1993 about becoming Minister of Education. (2) Dudley's recollections and reflections of a 1998 luncheon with President Mandela.

Richard Dudley had been very critical when people in the Unity Movement crossed to the United Democratic Front and eventually the African National Congress. We spoke of his analysis regarding Dullah Omar in the previous chapter. But it is also important to remember that according to Nasson, Omar brought many of the tenets of the Unity Movement to the ANC. Thus it was not a total surprise when Dullah Omar sent an emissary to meet with Dudley.

> The one thing that they did in my case—I got a call to say that they wanted to speak to me because they were eager to forward my name as Minister of Education. I would get the support of the people from

> the Unity Movement who were now sort of before court. That would have been round about 1993. This chap, Giyosi, whom they appointed to act as a go-between, is a fellow who I assisted to get on to his feet again, so they thought that he would be a good emissary. He was actually along with Omar and company preparing to take a position. Well I laughed. I said to this chap, I've been working in politics for a long time and I probably know all the problems in education. I also know that what they are doing now is not going to help solve the problems in education. So I'm not going to enter any job that I know that I must fail from day one. I said besides that you're asking me to collaborate with the collaborators. (Dudley Interview, 2003)

Richard Dudley was not the only person approached by the ANC in 1993 regarding the post of Minister of Education. For example, Neville Alexander was also queried regarding his interest. Knowing both Dudley's and Alexander's politics and intellect as well as the ANC's ultimate choice for the position, Professor Sibusiso Bengu, one has to question whether or not Dudley and Alexander were being seriously considered.

The topic was nonracialism when the Richard and Iris Dudley met with President Mandela in 1998. I must mention at this point, although somewhat tangentially, that it was Iris Dudley, not Richard Dudley, who first told me about the luncheon. She said that she was sure that he told me about having lunch with Mandela, and I had to answer NO. Just as I noted in Chapter Seven, Richard Dudley did not view it as an important event in his life. He did tell me the story, however. The approach was made by Virginia van Niekerk, President Mandela's personal secretary and a former Livingstone student, who invited Richard and Iris to have lunch with the President at Genadendal, the official presidential residence in Cape Town. The call came in the latter stages of 1998, preceding the 1999 elections in which the ANC was seeking to win a majority in the Western Cape, one of two provinces, the other being Kwazulu Natal, that the party did not win in 1994. The issue for the ANC in the Cape was winning the coloured vote, thus the invitation. Like all Unity Movement decisions, Dudley took the invitation before the board, where there were mixed feelings; some thought that they should dine with President Mandela, and others viewed it as collaboration. A decision was taken that the Dudleys would accept the president's invitation, and that meant that in spite of the fact that Nelson Mandela was well aware of Dudley's and the organization's definition of nonracialism, a lesson was forthcoming.

> Yes, we had lunch there. The one thing about that meeting was that he was extremely courteous. There was nothing, I would say, grating in the relationships that emerged from the very beginning right to

> the end. After having introduced ourselves, we spoke about the people in the Unity Movement with whom he was acquainted. He wanted to know about their health. He said to me that he knew that I was a very prominent person in the political field and that, well, I can't quote his exact words, but he said that I was a very prominent political . . . coloured political leader and so on, and he wanted to know whether it would be possible for us to make use of the influence that we had amongst the coloured people to secure their vote for the ANC. And he added that he found it very difficult to believe that the people could actually vote for a political party that had in the past been responsible for all the discriminatory legislation that had harmed the so-called coloured people for so long. And so he wanted the cooperation of myself and my comrades in getting in the vote for the ANC. He wanted to know whether I was prepared to give some help. So I said to him, now look, in the first place I am not a coloured person. I said that other people have classified me as that but I am not a coloured person. I am not a coloured leader. I said that I had for the past fifty years been associated with a political movement that does not accept these classifications, and has consistently fought to unify the people in this country and to establish a South Africa where such things are completely irrelevant. So I said that I understand what you have said, and how you have described me, but I said that I would like to make it plain that I am not a coloured leader, and I said now what actually happens then is that when I approach people, I approach them as a nonracial, nonsexist, and an individual totally committed to policies of the Unity Movement. And I said that this brings us into conflict with the ANC. I said to him that I will never, never surrender the political position that I have been supporting for the past fifty years. I will never want people to vote as coloured persons. I said I appeal to them to vote for a completely nonracial South Africa, and I would ask them not to give their support to any political party that does not accept the fact that there can only be one solution for all the people in this country. In any event, he said that he understood readily what I was telling him, and he was satisfied that I had spoken candidly in regard to this. (Dudley Interview, 2003)

So even in the company of the great man, Richard Dudley spoke nonracialism and was a teacher. Because his teaching and politics are forever intertwined, he as well as many of his Unity Movement comrades, while not current South African players, continue to affect ideas and issues and to confront present-day imperialism and class disparity. Whether or not Dudley and his comrades have any educational or political influence at the present moment is better understood within the context of the struggle years as recent history.

Thus it is time to return to Linda Chisholm's criticism that the Unity Movement lost the students in the 1980s.

Chisholm does give credence to the educational impact of Unity Movement teachers and also admits that there is a lasting political effect from the teachings of people like Richard Dudley. However, more than once in her article on the Unity Movement she argues that the organization lost its influence on students after the 1976 Soweto riots. But what does it mean to lose the students? Did many young people take a more activist stance during the struggle years? Yes. Did many young people leave the recreated fellowships and join the United Democratic Front? Yes. Did many young teachers not follow their teachers, parents, uncles, and aunts into the Teachers' League of South Africa, choosing the more activist South African Democratic Teachers Union? Yes. Conceding all of the above points, I want to suggest that the political teachings of Dudley and many of his comrades helped young people involved in the struggle conceptualize their actions. The politics they learned from Unity Movement teachers, especially people like Richard Dudley, provided the impetus that sent them marching and protesting and fighting for democracy. In fact, it was the teachings of Teachers' Leaguers like Dudley, in spite of their continual preaching of education for democracy rather than liberation before education that taught activist student leaders and young teachers the anti-imperialism and nonracialism that was the foundation of their activism. Although William Nasson thoughtfully challenges the Unity Movement, he makes a similar argument in "The Unity Movement: Its Legacy in Historical Consciousness."

> Yet the fracturing of Unity Movement leadership and its derisory significance in the world of South African exile politics did not erase its fecund deposit in the historical consciousness and levelling doctrines of professionals, students, and other adherents through the 1960s and 1970s. And, retaining some impetus on the left in the struggles and repression of the 1980s, new bodies consciously derived from the NEUM position have arisen in Cape Town to try to apply its customary principles and tactics to the strategies of the democratic movement. (Nasson, 1990, p. 195)

Dudley's influence, however, goes beyond principles and tactics. Nasson explains that the Unity Movement's "claim to being an authentic and distinctive national liberation movement rested more in the power of its ideas and arguments than in its organizational strength" (Nasson, 1990, p. 211). While there is truth to both parts of Nasson's analysis, there is more to capturing Richard Dudley's significance to the struggle for democracy in South Africa. As I began to conceptualize my original oral history project with South African teachers, colleagues at both the University of the Western Cape and the University of Cape Town explained that Richard Dudley was essential to the project. Professors who were not affiliated with the Unity Movement, and some who were, quickly brought up particular speeches that they would never forget; the Livingstone farewell speech and the UCT panel were often mentioned. Teachers from throughout the city told me that I must speak with Dudley. The words of many of Dudley's colleagues and comrades have already been conveyed, and Rose Jackson's quiet reference to the "benign Dudley spirit" speaks powerfully to the tone Dudley set at Livingstone—educationally and politically. While students often mentioned particular teachers at the school whom they viewed as mentors—Allie Fataar, Hendrik Esterhuzien, Stella Petersen, John Burch, Ray Carlier, Tessa Fairburn, Faiza Bardien, Simon Banda, and more; they always added that the heart of the school, both academically and politically, was Richard Dudley.

Both inside and outside of Livingstone High School, Dudley represented the best of the Unity Movement and the reality that democracy rests within the hands of human beings. His life with his students and colleagues, as well as others as will be addressed below, is an example of Martin Buber's relational thesis—*I and Thou*. While Buber acknowledges objects, called "It," he emphasizes that the essential human qualities occur through relationships with subjects, called "Thou." Dudley had the same understanding, and it is portrayed in his Livingstone farewell speech.

> No teacher can survive without the stimulation that he receives from these pupils. And I have enjoyed that stimulation over a long period of time. The young people at Livingstone have, I think, kept me in a state of rejuvenation. They have provided me with an opportunity of making contact with youthfulness, with vitality, with young ideas, good ideas, attractive ideas, stimulating ideas, worrying ideas and sometime very crummy ideas as well. And I will thank them for that stimulation—it has been an essential part of my luck that I should have met these people during my course of teaching. I want also to thank the many parents with whom I came into contact. Some of them expected me to perform miracles. I never claimed that I could but out of loyalty I did try. Others accepted that teaching was a hard job and adopted a more sympathetic approach to myself and of course to my colleagues at Livingstone. I want to thank them for all that they have meant. And then because the school has had such a long history there has been a regular band of persons who have backed up the school and very often in the most trying circumstances. They have provided me and others with a glimpse of the kind of service that a school needs to survive. They have done Livingstone proud in helping us to defend its traditions, to defend its staff, and to defend the pupils against the vandals, official and otherwise, who tried to turn Livingstone into a so called coloured school. None of us at that school have ever accepted that

> prescription for the school. And it is because we have constantly tried to maintain Livingstone as an educational institution which is willing to serve whoever comes. (Dudley, Livingstone High School Farewell Speech, 1984)

The "benign Dudley spirit" as well as his continuing way of living life relationally transcends the walls of Livingstone High School. As we have already noted many times throughout the text, Richard Dudley was a teacher in each and every situation. Simon Banda explained the breadth of Dudley's relationships:

> He dealt with a host of social, personal issues. Various facets that affected the lives of the people, he was consulted on. Be it monetary, be it personal conflicts, he was there, a person to whom people generally went, and I am not talking about the school alone, but within the community, the Claremont community, he was regarded as such a rich source of knowledge, of assistance, and despite his very incisive thinking ability, he also could relate to the simplest person. It wasn't odd, for example, to see one of the local beggars coming to school to see Mr. Dudley. (Banda Interview, 2003)

Whether it was family, students, comrades, colleagues, friends, neighbors, opposition, or school or government officials, life was teaching and life was relational for Richard Dudley. We remember that he spoke with both the communists and the brown shirts when he was a student at the University of Cape Town. At Livingstone High School he talked to Francke when no one else would acknowledge the man. He taught the train conductor who had him detained and the Education Department officials who threatened him. He lectured his interrogators on class disparity and racism when he was arrested in 1985. Richard Dudley knows that dialogue and the relationship between human beings leads to democratic possibilities. It was not coincidental that the ANC sent emissaries to Richard Dudley in an attempt to bring the Unity Movement into their fold in the early 1990s. Neither was it happenstance that they contacted him about the possibility of serving as the Minister of Education in 1993. And finally, when President Nelson Mandela called Richard and Iris Dudley to Genadendal to speak about the "coloured" vote, the president acted consciously. On each occasion, approaching Richard Dudley was not an accident because the African National Congress knew he would talk; they knew that he had lived his whole life believing that dialogue—talk with other human beings, even the opposition—had democratic possibilities. Not surprisingly, Dudley taught at each of the meetings, including his lunch with Mandela.

In an article titled, "Argument and History: What India's Modern Democracy Owes to its Ancient Culture of Disputation," Amartya Sen analyzes dialogue and democracy in India. As I read his account of Arjuna lecturing power in the *Bhagavad-Gita*, I could not help but think of Richard Dudley. Another scholar that comes to mind in referencing dialogue with power is the late Edward Said. Said's essay, "Speaking Truth to Power," argues that the role of the public intellectual is to advance ideas that are counter to the prevailing commonplaces. While Amartya Sen and Edward Said are very different politically, they both clearly understand that democracy demands "speaking back to power." So does Richard Dudley. Sen's work reminds me of Dudley because he addresses countervailing ideas and longevity. "We have to take note not only of the opinions that won (or allegedly won) in the disputations, but also of the other points of view that were presented and are recorded or remembered. A defeated argument that refuses to be obliterated can remain very much alive" (Sen, 2005, p. 26). Richard Dudley challenged power throughout the apartheid era, and if one believes as I do that his political teachings were foundational to anti-apartheid activists, then "a defeated argument that refuses to be obliterated can remain very much alive."

At the present time, as we have shown, Richard Dudley's foundational beliefs in nonracialism, anti-imperialism, and noncollaboration, as well as his living life in I-Thou relationships, mean that he continues to talk, teach, and speak to power. I would add that most importantly, Richard Dudley is a comrade and teacher.

glossary

African National Congress (ANC) was founded in 1912 and is currently the ruling party of South Africa. The ANC came of age in the 1950s through the leadership of Mandela, Tambo, and Sissulu. The organization was the leading force during the struggle years, entered negotiations with the apartheid government in the late 1980s, and assumed power in 1994.

African People's Democratic Union of South Africa (APDUSA) was launched by Tabata in 1961. He asserted that the organization would promote the Ten Point Programme and serve as the "military and political" arm of NEUM.

African Political Organization (APO) was formed in 1902 as an organization that fought for the rights of coloured people. The APO was more complex, however, as longtime leader Abdullah Abdurahman often sought alliances with black activists.

Afrikaners are the descendents of the seventeenth-century Dutch settlers in South Africa. They were defeated by the British in the early twentieth-century Boer War but came back to power very quickly. Afrikaners were the core of the apartheid ruling Nationalist Party.

All African Convention (AAC) was launched in response to Native Representative Councils in 1937. It was fairly dormant until it was revived and radicalized by Tabata and Gool in 1943.

Anti-CAD was formed in 1943 to fight the Coloured Affairs Department that was set up by the government. Members were interchangeable with NEUM and supported the latter group's programs.

Bantu Education Act was passed in 1953 and created separate and very unequal schools for black South Africans

Black Consciousness was a movement during the struggle years in South Africa that organized for black self-determination and provided an active voice for noncollaborative protest. The organization's best-known leader, Steve Biko, was murdered while in police custody.

Cape African Teachers' Association (CATA) was the African teachers union in Cape Town that cooperated closely with the TLSA.

Cape Professional Teachers Association (CPTA) was launched by conservative members of the TLSA when they broke away in 1944. The organization became much larger than the TLSA and attracted moderate and conservative teachers throughout the struggle years.

Christian National Education is an educational philosophy that became part of the apartheid school curriculum and stressed the intellectual and moral superiority of white people.

Coloured Affairs Department was initiated in 1943 to regulate issues relating to coloured South Africans.

Committee of Eighty-One was launched in 1980 as a Cape Town student organization that marched against apartheid and gutter education.

Congress of South African Trade Unions (COSATU) was started in 1985 as a unity organization that fought apartheid during the late struggle years and joined the ANC along with SACP as secondary partners in the first democratic government.

District Six is an area of Cape Town that was vibrant and interracial. The apartheid government used it as a public example of apartheid forced removals.

Educational Journal is the journal of the Teachers' League of South Africa, first published in 1915 and still published today. The journal includes educational and cultural news, issues and opinions, as well as philosophical discussions, debates, conference proceedings, grievances, curriculum, and model lessons.

Forced removals in the 1960s and 1970s followed the Group Areas Act (1950) as the government forced black people to leave their homes and relocate to racially designated neighborhoods.

Fourth International was founded in the 1940s as a Trotskyist opposition organization.

Freedom Charter was adopted by the ANC-led Congress on June 26, 1955, as a call for total equality in South Africa.

Group Areas Act was enacted in 1950. The law divided urban areas racially and led to forced removals of black people from their homes.

Gutter Education is a phrase used by activists to describe apartheid education.

Herrenvolk was the German concept of master race that was invoked by the Afrikaners.

Industrial and Commercial Union (ICU) was founded in 1919 to fight for the rights of workers and rural South Africans. The organization grew to over 100,000 people but expired in the 1930s.

Lenin Club began in the early 1930s in Cape Town as a Trotskyist nonracial discussion group. It organized various activities and events, including a socialist Sunday school for children, study groups, and a number of public political meetings.

Livingstone High School, Dudley's school, was founded in 1926 as a coloured high school and is known historically as well as presently as both an academic and political institution.

Nationalist Party is the political party that initiated apartheid in 1948 and ruled South Africa until 1994.

Natives Representative Council (NRC) was set up by the government as a divide-and-rule institution in the 1930s to represent Africans with white legislators.

National Union of South African Students (NUSAS) was a predominantly white student organization that opposed apartheid during the struggle years.

New Era Fellowship (NEF) was founded in Cape Town in 1937 as a sophisticated socialist debate society where issues of imperialism and capitalism were connected to inequality and racism in South Africa.

New Unity Movement (NUM) was launched by Dudley and his comrades in the early 1980s as a reinstitution of NEUM. The organization attempted to be an alternative to the ANC and UDF.

Non-European Unity Movement (NEUM) was launched in the early 1940s as part of the Anti-CAD. The organization was nonracial and noncollaborationist with an anti-imperialist and socialist mission.

Oorstroming was the apartheid word for flooding and was used in reference to African people coming into urban areas to find work. Besides Pass Laws, the Group Areas Act and African Homelands were apartheid segregation solutions intended to end oorstroming.

Pan African Congress (PAC) was an Africanist organization that was officially launched in 1959 by Robert Sobukwe. The organization led boycotts against the apartheid government, including Sharpeville.

Pass Laws Although African people were sometimes required to carry passes before apartheid, after 1948 the laws were intensified and black South Africans were not permitted to be in urban areas without government pass books. Large numbers of people were harassed and imprisoned for not having the proper documentation. Boycotts and marches were held to protest the laws, the most famous being Sharpeville.

Rivonia Trial After Sharpeville, the most visible portrait of apartheid oppression in the 1960s was the Rivonia Trial, where Nelson Mandela and ten comrades were brought to docket in 1964 for conspiracy, incitement, armed invasion, and violent revolution against the state of South Africa. All of the final defendants except Rusty Bernstein were convicted and sent to prison.

Robben Island was the prison where Nelson Mandela and other anti-apartheid political prisoners were sentenced to life with hard labor. Neville Alexander spent twelve years in the prison.

Sharpeville Massacre was precipitated when police shot into the crowds of thousands of people protesting Pass Laws in March 1960. Sixty-nine people were murdered by the police, many shot in their backs.

South African Committee on Sport (SACOS) was a nonracial sport group that boycotted segregated sport in South Africa under the banner "no normal sport in an abnormal society."

South African Democratic Teachers' Union (SADTU) is a national teachers union that was founded by activist and radical teachers in the 1980s.

South African Institute of Race Relations (SAIRR) is an organization that was founded in 1929 with the purpose of influencing government through research and suggestion, not politics.

South African Native National Congress (SANNC) began in 1912 and was the forerunner of today's presiding political party, the African National Congress.

South African Students' Organization (SASO) was started in 1969 when Biko and other black members of NUSAS left to form SASO, the foundational body of black consciousness in South Africa.

South African War, also referred to as the Boer War, was fought between British and Afrikaner troops at the turn of the twentieth century.

South Peninsula Educational Fellowship (SPEF) was a struggle years socialist debate society where issues of apartheid, imperialism, and capitalism were discussed and debated.

Student Representative Councils (SRC) were leadership student organizations in coloured schools in Cape Town. During the struggle there was a city-wide SRC.

Teachers' Action Committee (TAC) was started in 1980 by activist teachers. TAC was a short-lived group but marked the beginnings of an activist counterpoint to both conservative teachers and socialist Teachers' Leaguers.

Teachers' League of South Africa (TLSA) was launched in the early twentieth century as an advocate organization for coloured teachers. A schism in the early 1940s moved the organization to a more socialist, nonracial, and noncollaborationist mission.

Teacher Training Colleges were racially segregated institutions that students could enter after tenth grade to train as teachers.

The Torch was first published in 1946 in quiet cooperation with NEUM. The newspaper closed in 1964 when apartheid suppression accelerated in South Africa. *The Torch* was an eight-page publication named after the Bolshevik publication *Iskra*.

Transvaal African Teachers Association (TATA) was an African teacher organization in the Johannesburg area of South Africa that included the three teachers who were first banned by the apartheid government.

Truth and Reconciliation Commission was a government initiative where ethnic groups came together so that people could publicly tell their tragic stories of the oppression that they experienced at the hands of individuals and the apartheid state and where perpetrators could express remorse and ask for forgiveness. Chaired by Bishop Tutu, the TRC was an attempt at healing across South Africa.

Umkhonto we Sizwe (Spear of the Nation, referred to as MK) was the military wing of the ANC.

United Democratic Front (UDF) was launched in 1983 as a nonracial opposition group that took the protests against apartheid to the streets throughout South Africa.

Western Cape Teachers Union (WECTU) was founded by anti-apartheid activists in Cape Town in the early 1980s. WECTU was the forerunner of SADTU.

Yui Chui Chan Club/National Liberation Front was a militant anti-apartheid group that was founded by Neville Alexander and Kenneth Abrahams in the early 1960s.

sources

Interviews (with author, 1999–2005)

1999

Neville Alexander
Jeff Cohen
Tom Hanmer
Sedick Issacs
Beth Mclagan
Jean September
Glen van Harte
June Bam
Pam Dewes
Anthony Hess
Rose Jackson
Dennis Ntombela
Jimmy Slingers
Kevin Wildschut
Vivienne Carelse
Richard Dudley
Pam Hicks
Helen Kies
Mandy Sanger
Polly Slingers

2001

Richard Dudley

2002

Richard Dudley

2003

Albert Adams
Simon Banda
Albert Clarke
Gary Dudley
Russell Dudley
Ralph Freese
Arthur Hendricks
Robin Hendricks
Rose Jackson
William Nasson
Ernest Steenberg
Abjurahman Ajam
Faiza Bardien
Yusuf da Costa
Iris Dudley
Tessa Fairbairn
Jonathan Fry
Paul Hendricks
Pam Hicks
Goolam Jaffers
Stella Petersen
Kathy Steenberg
Azeem Badroodien
Malcolm Campbell
Pam Dewes
Richard Dudley
Allie Fataar
Sean Goldschmidt
Rhoda Hendricks
Zane Ibrahim
Alan Liebenberg
Ebrahim Rassool

2005

Richard Dudley

Pamphlets and Unpublished Sources

Alexander, Neville (Mildred Poswa). TLSA. (1982) *Black Consciousness: A Reactionary Tendency*. Cape Town.

Dudley, Richard. TLSA. (1955). *The Control of the Parent: Bantu Authorities, School Committees, School Boards*. Cape Town: Dudley, Richard.

Dudley, Richard. NUM. (1987). *New Unity Movement Bulletin*. Cape Town.

Dudley, Richard. APDUSA. (1988). Foreword—300 Years" by Hosea Jaffe. Cape Town.

Dudley, Richard. NUM. (1989). *Negotiations: The Road to Betrayal*. Cape Town.

Dudley, Richard. NUM. (1991). *The Revolutionary Road to Liberation*. Cape Town.

Dudley, Richard. NUM. (1992). *Jonas Fred Bosch Memorial Lecture*. Cape Town.

Dudley, Richard. NUM. (1992). *New Unity Movement Presidential Address*. Cape Town.

Dudley, Richard. NUM. (1993) *50th Year of Struggle: And the Struggle Continues*. Cape Town.

Dudley, Richard. NUM. (1998). *New Unity Movement Presidential Address*. Cape Town.

Dudley, Richard. Ray Carlier Eulogy. (1998). Cape Town.

Dudley, Richard. *Commentary on The School Creed*. (1999). Cape Town.

Dudley, Richard. *Harvey Hendricks Eulogy*. (1999). Cape Town.

Dudley, Richard. *Zantsi Mzimba Eulogy*. (2001). Cape Town.

Dudley, Richard. *Book Launch Address at UWC* (2003). Cape Town.

Dudley, Richard. NUM. (2003). *The Dumbing of South Africa*. Cape Town.

Jaffe, Hosea. NUM. (1992). *The Contribution of the Europeans to World Civilization*. Cape Town.

Kies, Ben. APDUSA. (nd). *The Background of Segregation*. Cape Town.

Kies, Ben. TLSA. (nd). *The Contribution of the Non European Peoples to World Civilisation*. Cape Town.

Livingstone High School. (1996). *Founders' Day Celebration Programme*. Cape Town.

Livingstone High School. (1967). *The School Creed*. Cape Town.

Mokone, Sarah. TLSA. (1991). *Majority Rule: Some Notes*. Cape Town.

NUM. (1993) *Elections '94*. Cape Town.

NUM. (1993) *The Lessons of June 16, 1976*. Cape Town.

Van Schoor, Willem. "The Origin and Development of Segregation in South Africa," Cape Town, APDUSA, 1986.

Books, Chapters, Articles, Dissertation

Abrahams, Peter. (1954). *Tell Freedom*. New York: Alfred Knopf.

Adhikari, Mohamed. (1993). *Let Us Live for Our Children: The Teachers' League of South Africa*, 1913–1940. Cape Town: UCT Press.

Adhikari, Mohamed. (2005). *Beyond Black and White: Racial Identity in the South African Coloured Community*. Athens: Ohio University Press.

Alexander, Neville. (1979). *One Azania, One Nation*. London: Zed Press.

Alexander, Neville. (1989). Non-Collaboration in the Western Cape. In James Wilmot, and Mary Simons (Eds.), *The Angry Divide*. Cape Town: David Philip.

Alexander, Neville. (2002). *An Ordinary Country*. Pietermaritzburg: University of Natal Press.

Anderson, Gregory. (2002) *Building a People's University in South Africa: Race, Compensatory Education, and the Limits of Democratic Reform*. New York: Peter Lang.

Bickford-Smith, Vivian. (2001) Mapping Cape Town: From Slavery to Apartheid. In Sean Field, *Lost Communities, Living Memories*. Cape Town: David Philip.

Bickford-Smith, Vivian, Elizabeth van Heyningen, and Nigel Worden. (1999) *Cape Town in the Twentieth Century*. Cape Town: David Philip.

Beinart, William. (1994). *Twentieth-Century South Africa*. Oxford: Oxford University Press.

Biko, Steve. (1971). "The Definition of Black Consciousness." SASO.

Biko, Steve. (1978). *I Write What I Like*. San Francisco: Harper and Row Publishers.

Brink, Andre. (1998) *Reinventing a Continent: Writing and Politics in South Africa*. Cambridge: Zoland Books.

Chisholm, Linda. (1991). Education, Politics and Organisation: The Educational Traditions and Legacies of the Non-European Unity Movement 1943–86. *Transformation* 15. pp. 1–25.

Cleaver, Kathleen and George Katsiaficas (2001). *Liberation, Imagination, and the Black Panther Party*. New York: Routledge.

Constas, Mark. (1996) Apartheid and the Socio-Political Context of Education in South Africa: A Narrative Account. *Teachers College Record*. (Fall) 1–39.

Curry, Constance, Joan Browning, Dorothy Burlage, Penny Patch, Theresa del Pozzo, Sue Thrasher, Elaine Baker, Emmie Adams, and Casey Hayden (2000). *Deep in Our Hearts: Nine White Women in the Freedom Movement*. Athens: University of Georgia Press.

DeVilliers, Elizabeth. (1990). *Walking the Tightrope: Recollections of a Schoolteacher in Soweto*. Johannesburg: Jonathan Ball.

Drew, Allison. (2002). *Discordant Comrades: Identitites and Loyalties on the South African Left*. Pretoria: UNISA Press.

Dubow, Saul. (1989). *Racial Segregation and the Origins of Apartheid in South Africa, 1919–36*. London: MacMillan.

Dubow, Saul. (2000). *The African National Congress*. Johannesburg: Jonathan Ball.

Dudley, Richard. (1948). About Ourselves—Then and Now. *Educational Journal*. (September, October) pp. 2–4.

Dudley, Richard. (1948). A Little Learning. *Educational Journal*. (March) p. 3.

Dudley, Richard. (1951). Advice to the Beginning Teacher. *Educational Journal*. (November/December) pp. 8–9.

Dudley, Richard. (1952). Scholarship and Scholasticism. *Educational Journal*. (March) pp. 6–7.

Dudley, Richard. (1953). The Bantu Education Bill. *Educational Journal*. (September) pp. 5–6.

Dudley, Richard. (1953). The Burden of Coloured Education. *Educational Journal*. (March) pp. 3–4.

Dudley, Richard. (1990). Forced Removals: The Essential Meanings of District Six. In Shamil Jeppie and Crain Soudien, *The Struggle for District Six*. Cape Town: Buchu Books.

Fanon, Frantz. (1967). *Black Skin White Masks*. New York: Grove Press.

Finnegan, William. (1994). *Crossing the Line: A Year in the Land of Apartheid*. Berkeley: University of California Press.

Frankel, Glenn. (1999). *Rivonia's Children*. New York: Farrar, Straus and Giroux.

Gilroy, Paul. (2000). *Against Race*. Cambridge: Harvard University Press.

Goldin, Ian. (1987). *Making Race: The Politics and Economics of Coloured Identity in South Africa*. London: Longman.

Goodson, Ivor. (1996). The Life and Work of Teachers. *South African Review of Education*. (V2, N2) pp. 1–19.
Hommel, Maurice. (1981). *Capricorn Blues: The Struggle for Human Rights in South Africa.* Toronto: Culturama.
Hugo, Pierre. (1978). *Quislings or Realists? A Documentary Study of 'Coloured' Politics in South Africa.* Johannesburg: Raven Press.
Hyslop, Jonathan. (1999). *The Classroom Struggle: Policy and Resistance in South Africa 1940–1990.* Pietermaritzburg: University of Natal Press.
James, Wilmot & Mary Simons. (1989). *The Angry Divide: Social and Economic History of the Western Cape.* Cape Town: David Philip.
Jeppie, Shamil and Crain Soudien. (1990). *The Struggle for District Six.* Cape Town: Buchu Books.
Kallaway, Peter. (1984). *Apartheid and Education: The Education of Black South Africans.* Johannesburg: Raven Press.
Kallaway, Peter. (2002). *The History of Education Under Apartheid.* New York: Peter Lang.
Kallaway, Peter. (2005). Welfare and Education in British Colonial Africa and South Africa during the 1930s and 1940s. *Paedagogica Historica.* (June) pp. 337–356.
Karis, Thomas and Gwendolen Carter. (1972). *From Protest to Challenge: A Documentary History of African Politics in South Africa 1882–1964.* Stanford: Hoover Institution Press, V1.
Karis, Thomas and Gwendolen Carter. (1973). *From Protest to Challenge: A Documentary History of African Politics in South Africa 1882–1964.* Stanford: Hoover Institution Press, V2.
Karis, Thomas and Gwendolen Carter. (1977). *From Protest to Challenge: A Documentary History of African Politics in South Africa 1882–1964.* Stanford: Hoover Institution Press, V3.
Karis, Thomas and Gwendolen Carter. (1977). *From Protest to Challenge: A Documentary History of African Politics in South Africa 1882–1964.* Stanford: Hoover Institution Press, V4.
Karis, Thomasand Gail Gerhart. (1977). *From Protest to Challenge: A Documentary History of African Politics in South Africa 1882–1964.* Stanford: Hoover Institution Press, V5.
Kihn, Paul. (2002). Comrades and Professionals: Teacher Ideology and Practices in the Western Cape, 1985 to 1990. In Kallaway, Peter. *The History of Education Under Apartheid.* New York: Peter Lang.
Lewis, Gavin. (1987). *Between the Wire and the Wall: A History of South African Coloured Politics.* Cape Town: Johannesburg, David Philip.
Lodge, Tom and William Nasson. (1991). *All, Here, and Now: Black Politics in South Africa in the 1980s.* Cape Town: David Philip.
Mandela, Nelson. (2001). *Long Walk to Freedom.* South Africa: Macdonald Purnell.
Marais, Hein. (2001) *South Africa: Limits to Change.* London, Cape Town: Zed Books, University of Cape Town Press.
Matthews, Zachariah. (1990). *Freedom for My People.* Cape Town: David Philip.
Meli, Francis. (1998). *A History of the ANC: South Africa Belong to Us.* Harare, Bloomington, London: Zimbawe Publishing House, Indiana University Press, James Currey.
Molteno, Frank. (1987). *Students Struggle for Their Schools.* Cape Town: The Centre for African Studies.
Mphahlele, Eskia. (1978). *Down Second Avenue: Growing Up in a South African Ghetto.* Gloucester, MA: Peter Smith.

Nasson, Bill. (1990). The Unity Movement: Its Legacy in Historical Consciousness. *Radical History Review*. pp. 189–211.

Ndlovu, Sifiso. (1998). *The Soweto Uprisings: Counter-Memories of June 1976*. Johannesburg: Raven Press.

Paton, Alan. (1964). *Hofmeyr*. Cape Town: Oxford University Press.

Plaatje, Solomon. (2004). *Native Life in South Africa*. New York: Kessinger.

Poswa, Mildred. (1976). "Black Consciousness: A Reactionary Tendency." *The Educational Journal*.

Rassool, Ciraj. (2004). The Individual, Auto/biography and History in South Africa. Cape Town: University of the Western Cape. (Ph.D. Dissertation).

Rassool, Joe. (2000). *District Six—Lest We Forget*. Cape Town: University of Western Cape.

Reid, Graeme and Liz Walker. (2005). *Men behaving differently: South African men since 1994*, Cape Town: Double Storey Books.

Rive, Richard. (1964). *Emergency*. Cape Town: David Philip.

Rive, Richard. (1990). *Emergency Continued*. Cape Town: David Philip.

Rive, Richard and Tim Couzens. (1993). *Seme: Founder of the ANC*. Trenton: African World Press.

Roux, Eddie. (1967). *Time Longer Than Rope*. Madison: University of Wisconsin Press.

Said, Edward. (1994). *Representations of the Intellectual*. New York: Pantheon.

Saunders, Christopher. (1988). *The Making of the South African Past: Major Historians on Race and Class*. Totowa, NJ: Barnes & Noble Books.

Seekings, Jeremy. (2000). *The UDF: A History of the United Democratic Front in South Africa 1983–1991*. Cape Town, Oxford, Athens: David Philip, James Currey, Ohio University Press.

Sen, Amartya. (2005). Argument and History: What India's Modern Democracy Owes to its Ancient Culture of Disputation. *New Republic*. (August 8).

Simons, Jack & Ray Simons. (1983). *Class and Colour in South Africa 1850–1950*. Berne: IDAF.

Tabata, Isaac. (1959). *Education for Barbarism*. London: Prometheus.

Terreblanche, Solomon. (2002). *History of Inequality in South Africa*, Pietermaritzburg: University of Natal Press.

Thompson, Leonard. (2000). *A History of South Africa*. New Haven: Yale University Press.

Tutu, Desmond. (1999). *No Future Without Forgiveness*. New York: Image/Doubleday.

Western, John. (1996). *Outcast Cape Town*. Berkeley: University of California Press.

Wieder, Alan. (2003). *Voices from Cape Town Classrooms: Oral Histories of Teachers Who Fought Apartheid*. New York: Peter Lang.

Willemse, Hein. (2000). *More Than Brothers*. Cape Town: Kwela Books.

Witz, Leslie. (2003). *Apartheid's Festival: Contesting South Africa's National Pasts*. Bloomington: Indiana University Press.

Witz, Leslie. (1998/99) From Langa Market Hall and Rhodes' Estate to the Grand Parade and the Foreshore: Contesting Van Riebeeck's Cape Town. *Kronos*. pp. 187–206.

index